TRANSIT LOUNGE

An Indian's account of travelling to thirty
countries across six continents

Sunil Mishra

FROG BOOKS

ISBN 978-93-52017-15-7
Copyright © Sunil Mishra, 2018

First published in India 2018 by Frog Books
An imprint of Leadstart Publishing Pvt Ltd

Sales Office:
Unit No.25-26, Building No.A/1,
Near Wadala RTO,
Wadala (East), Mumbai – 400037 India
Phone: +91 96 99933000
Email: info@leadstartcorp.com
www.leadstartcorp.com

Disclaimer: The Views expressed in this book are those of the Author and do not pertain to be held by the Publisher.

Editor: Shilpi Sinha
Cover: Tina
Layouts: Logiciels Info Solutions Pvt. Ltd.

Printed at Repro

Dedication

I dedicate this book to my wife Archana who supported me during my hectic travel schedules for last many years. I also dedicate this book to my sons, Adithya and Vikesh. Their never ending curiosity about my experience of travelling to different countries, encouraged me to write this book.

CONTENTS

ABOUT THE AUTHOR

Sunil is a software professional with over two decades of experience in the field of banking technology. Currently he is working with Infosys in India. He has earlier worked with McKinsey, Accenture and I-flex solutions. His work required extensive travelling to different parts of the world and this constituted the basis of his current book. He travelled to more than 30 countries across six continents and engaged with senior managements in different client organizations. He believes that there has been a remarkable change in perception about india over last 15 years.

Sunil is an MBA from IIM-Lucknow and holds a B.Tech from UT(ISM), Dhanbad. He completed his schooling in Bokaro Steel City, a relatively small town in Jharkhand, India. Sunil has avid interest in writing and has actively blogged on various platforms in the area of banking technology, consulting, leadership and changing role of media in the digital world.

Twitter - @mishraksunil
LinkedIn- /in/sunilkrmishra
Facebook - ©authorsunil

ACKNOWLEDGEMENTS

I want to thank my employer Infosys for providing me with the opportunities to visit some of the most exotic countries in the world. Most IT professionals in India travel predominantly to countries like US, UK, Singapore and Australia etc., I was fortunate to travel to many other countries in the last 15 years, for short and long durations and I absolutely loved this part of my work which gave me an opportunity to learn and write about the experiences in different countries.

I used to write personal notes of the individual travels, anything that I would find interesting. I want to thank my wife Archana, who encouraged me to write a blog about some of these travels. As I started blogging about some of these travels, I received positive reviews from my friends and well-wishers. It is then that the idea of collating this and publishing it as a book occurred to me. I am extremely thankful to my friends who helped me overcome the initial hesitation and inertia to write this book.

Finally, I was told that publishers do not publish a memoir unless the writer is famous. My first reach-out to several mainstream publishers, way back in 2010, to publish this book was not quite successful. I am thankful to Leadstart publishing - Uzair Thakur and Shilpi Sinha for providing necessary support and guidance in publishing of this book.

PREFACE

"Transit Lounge" is a contemporary book consisting of short incidents, observations and reflections while travelling to 30 countries across six different continents during the last 15 years.

The book is a personal account of travels to places in Africa (Nigeria, Ghana, Egypt and Mauritius), South America (Venezuela and Argentina), Asia (China, Iran, Kuwait, UAE, Singapore, Indonesia, Sri Lanka, Malaysia and Thailand), Europe (UK, France, Italy, Netherlands, Germany, Denmark, Belgium, Georgia, Turkey, Croatia and Romania), USA, Australia and New Zealand. It was interesting to observe all these different cultures and people from an Indian perspective. The book is a compilation of small incidents and events during such travels; it includes losing an air ticket, dealing with difficult custom officials or getting mugged in a prime location in a foreign country. It is based on observations that someone with an Indian context will find most noticeable while talking to a taxi driver, walking through the local markets or going to a tourist destination. In essence, it is about an Indian travelling the world and discovering India in the process.

The last decade has also seen fast growth in India and a mixed acknowledgement of the same from the world. During these travels over last fifteen years, I was also witness to the change in perception in the developed countries towards growing Indian outsourcing industry - from cheap labor to a cost effective value destination, something that has helped India create a USD 150 billion IT industry today. Even though this industry is facing disruption now, it has helped India place itself prominently on the world map. The Indian migrants in all these countries have also seen a marked change in the way they connect with their erstwhile homeland and their own self-image. Though not explicit, this book is in a backdrop of exponential rise in india's economic position so it has some elements of growth stories as well. In part, this book is an account of various cultures, religions, economic aspects and anything that is most visible at the first sight for an Indian visitor.

This book is not a tourist's analysis on figures and facts - it is less informative in that sense. It is more on observations, interpretations and at times, opinions. Given the large scope, there is good likelihood that some observations could be partial, in pockets, non-exhaustive and selective extrapolation. This book is a non-expert's account of capturing the world view from personal experiences of travelling. It is in no way an attempt to capture the complete story, it is rather a series of incomplete observations as in a traveler's account. I still think they make sense as many of you would relate to the incidents and appreciate the point of view.

I think it will be interesting for the readers as they could relate to some of these experiences in their own context. It is nice at times, to go back in memory, reflect on the travel incidents and experiences. All of us have fond memories as travelers. I thought it could be a nice idea to create a platform for sharing those memorable experiences. The Facebook page - https://www.facebook.com/AuthorSunil/ is an attempt in that direction. Other than providing feedback, the readers can reflect on the incidents that are similar to or different from the book, share photographs or describe anything related to their travel. I will be happy to add some of these incidents in the subsequent additions of the book . As in my case, I believe a non expert's account is sometime more authentic and interesting.

International travel from India - Then and Now

Those of us who undertook international travel during late nineties would recall how things have changed over last 20 years. The travel itself used to be an adventure. Most of the international flights would only take off from Mumbai or Delhi. The flight timings would usually be odd (something like 4:30 am in the morning). I never understood why international flights from India had such weird timing those days. Such timing meant that we had to travel from Bangalore one night before and spend the early hours half asleep. The airport transfer bus at Mumbai (from domestic to international) airport used to be another adventure which had its own long queues and rules. This transit facility operated by the government captured the plight of the fliers. At any point of time one would see numerous fliers pleading with the security personnel to get them ahead in the queue as they would miss their international flight otherwise. The security personnel had a solution always - take the private taxi from outside. The private taxi guys fully exploited the situation by charging the fare in multiples.

Then there used to be the long queues for check-ins where we had to wait for hours. That space used to be very crowded, noisy and at times full with mosquitoes and flies. Finding a place to sit, whether in the boarding area or the check-in area was more of a musical chair. Those international travels had the potential to make any healthy person sick even before the journey started. Custom clearance used to be another fearful exercise, especially since I was carrying two laptops most of times for business purposes. Carrying two laptop was almost criminal those days - the custom guy would take me to a separate room and ask scores of questions. Even though I had all the official papers, every time a different custom officer handled it differently; there was no standard operating procedure for this. I think the custom officers were always trained to ask weird questions like *"why are you in such a business that requires carrying two laptops?"*

Finally the boarding process - there used to another big queue. This queue baffled many - why such a long queue before boarding the aircraft, after all everyone had a seat reserved and the flight would not leave before everyone was on board. However it was not unusual to see all the fliers waiting in the boarding queue for more than an hour. Someone told me once that such queues were more in India because Indians still thought of flights more like a bus; as in a bus when it gets full others can't get seat or board. They forgot often that in the flight everyone surely had a seat reserved and there was no need to rush. The ordeal continued till the flight would take off.

The experience between the Indian airports and any other international airport in Europe or US was so vastly different that I never thought the Indian airports would ever catch-up in our lifetime. Even the airports in other South East Asian countries like Singapore, HK and Malaysia used to be world apart. Every time I landed in Singapore and compared my experience in Mumbai or Delhi - I realized why Indians never wanted to go back to their own country once they went abroad; it was an escape from the crowd, the airlines, the custom officers and everything. I wonder what the foreigners would have felt those days travelling to India. I am sure many of them would have written a book when they first visited a country of snake charmers. If one had to guess the state of the country from the condition of India's airport and airlines, it was nothing short of disaster in 1990s or early 2000s. As per a world ranking from Forbes in 2009, 3 of the top five worst airports in the world were in India - Mumbai topped the list, Delhi on 3rd and Bangalore on 5th.

The arrivals at the airports were no better. I remember once we went to receive some of our colleagues from Singapore at Bangalore airport (now old airport). They were visiting India for the first time in 2006. We saw them coming out of the arrival area and then going back thrice. Later when we asked them - they said when they came out to see the huge crowd stepping on each other with multiple placards in their hand, they guessed there was some commotion and went back to safety. Only later they were told, this was the usual scene at the arrival area at Indian airports. The taxi drivers would vie with each other, at times take your luggage (almost snatch) and charge exorbitant amounts - there was hardly a concept of pre-paid taxis.

Having said all the above, it is also remarkable how quickly the infrastructure at Indian airports have changed in the last 15 years. When today we land at T3 in Delhi, it is no way different from Singapore anymore. The vast open space, automatic baggage handling, selfcheck-in kiosk and sprawling shopping area - almost all the Indian airports today are vying for the best infrastructure in the world. In 2017, Airport council international ranked many of the India's airport among the best in world (Hyderabad at the first position, Delhi at number 2) as per service quality passenger survey. Airports at Mumbai and Bengaluru among many others today can boast of world class facilities as well. Though Air India continues to be rated as third worst airlines, Indians are not complaining as they have several other Indian and international airlines. If the airports told a story - India has a turnaround and a remarkable turnaround in a very short time.

The world of travel has changed for good as well. We all remember the booklet like air ticket with red colored page. It was the most precious possession, as important as the passport during the travel. Our next generation would never believe such a thing ever existed, just like a typewriter in today's world of computers.

Chapters Outline

Chapter 1 - Africa - Starting with the most memorable trips

Countries: Ghana, Nigeria, Egypt, Mauritius

This chapter starts with the anxiety of my first international travel in early 2000 when I found it was so difficult to clear immigration in Mumbai. Based on my seven month's stay, it covers the life in Ghana and Nigeria. It touches on the cultural aspects, economic prospects and Indian immigrants there. Description of Egypt is more from a tourist perspective; first when I visited earlier and later again when I revisited after 9 years with a pretty different perspective. I travelled to Mauritius multiple times for short visits.

Chapter 2 - Middle-East Asia, some little travelled destinations

Countries: Iran, Kuwait, UAE, Turkey

My travel to Tehran is the most exotic in this section. For Tehran, this section explores the similarity of culture with the Indian culture impact of the Islamic revolution, general social conditions and anti-Americanism to some extent. Kuwait and UAE are described as a typical middle-east country - wealth for the local Arabs, state of Indian migrants etc. Turkey though is technically part of Europe, it has strong Asian links and hence covered in this section. It is practically a living example of Islam and Christianity having co-existed from historical perspective and this section dwells on the same among few other things.

Chapter 3 - United States of America - one of the most common destinations for Indians

Countries: USA

This section covers multiple trips and short stays at different cities in US during 2004- 2006. The first trip starts with the incident of losing the air tickets on- way and subsequent handling of the same. It covers the life in general there, the economic prosperity and the subsequent recession that followed. It tries to capture in parts - how a typical Indian migrant adapts to the conditions there and how it has changed so rapidly in the last 10 years. It also touches on things like outsourcing using some incidents and reflections.

Chapter 4 - Western Europe - Growth & prosperity of the past decades

Countries: UK, Netherlands, Belgium, Italy, France, Germany, Denmark

This section covers multiple countries from economic, social and lifestyle perspectives. Many are a tourist's accounts of some beautiful places like Venice and Amsterdam. Among many others, it includes incident of getting mugged in a prime location in London and description of the beautiful canals of Amsterdam. Amongst the wealth and prosperity, it tries to interpret the Indian immigrant's life in some of these countries.

Chapter 5 - Eastern Europe - Similar but fragmented

Countries: Croatia, Romania, Georgia

These are the tourist's accounts of places still in Europe but so different and quite fragmented. Croatia is a beautiful country to tour. The incidents cover one night of pub hopping in Bucharest and meeting with a vivacious Indian origin person. Many of these countries have been erstwhile communist regimes and that is still visible in many ways. A little known beautiful city called Tbilisi in Georgia, is described from a little bit cultural and tourist perspective.

Chapter 6 - Australia & New Zealand - Gifted with abundance & natural beauty

Countries: Australia, New Zealand

New Zealand is one of the most scenic places described in this book. During multiple visits to Auckland and Wellington, it covers the life there in general. It starts with the perspective of a Pakistani taxi driver who went there for higher studies and after completing, got into taxi driving. Australia, much bigger and richer in wild life and nature is described from the social and cultural aspect as well.

Chapter 7 - Asian region with city states - Emerging nations on the world stage

Countries: Singapore, Malaysia, Thailand, Indonesia, Hong Kong, China, Sri Lanka

I stayed in Singapore for two years, so it is more of resident's account of life and work there. The orderly and systematic lifestyle there, first starts with awe and praise but quickly sinks into a sense of synthetic beauty. Indonesia and Malaysia are touched upon briefly from tourism and social life perspective. Hong Kong and China are covered as experiential accounts of multiple travels.

Chapter 8 - Latin America - Yet to be discovered by Indians

Countries: Argentina, Venezuela

It surprised me the most because I knew about Latin America the least. The vibrant night life in Buenos-Aires and the partying culture - starting Thursday with a notion of weekend, were notable. The place seemed most alien to me as an Indian, hence it was not surprising that I hardly found any Indians there. Venezuela - famous for its Miss World title winners also had some good touring places. It was a discovery for me, that their culture is one of the most open one compared to many other western countries.

Chapter 1

Africa - Starting with the memorable trips

Ghana

It was my first international travel in early 2000. No one congratulated me on hearing the destination. In our heads it was Africa - Ghana. Many understood it to be one of those hazards of professional life - who would rest his case for an African country when sought after destinations for Indian software professionals were havens like US or Europe. To be honest, I took it as a professional compulsion too. But now, after so many years of travel, my view has changed. It was one of the most memorable destinations to talk about. People are generally biased and prejudiced when it comes to Africa.

The preparation of the travel included taking a vaccine of Yellow Fever which can be scary enough for the uninitiated. I had also heard that Malaria was still quite common those days - and almost all our colleagues had got it once at least. I was wondering - am I going to a place where the mosquitoes and insects still rule human habitat? I learned that though Yellow Fever vaccine was available, there was no vaccine against Malaria. I braced myself for Malaria - I was told it was not life threatening anyway. The symptoms did seem scary though (high fever at night). I must say our Indian upbringing sometimes prepares us for not-so-great living conditions, the only difference was unfamiliarity with African mosquitoes.

Mumbai (Bombay then) was never to be presumed for being kind to the international travelers, more so those days. The custom officials looked at every person going abroad as their possible fortune. They must have had a sure shot mechanism to identify the first-time-traveler to target specifically. Whatever way, they netted me spot on. The custom officer while checking my passport asked for the Yellow Fever card, which I obediently handed over. He pointed out that I should have taken the vaccine at least 7 days before travel. I was not aware of the same. He presented this as very big problem at that time - enough to make me worried. All my claims of ignorance were quashed and he kind of ruled out my travel further. Before I could look for any solution - he had one already. He suggested, if I pay him half of what I was carrying as cash it should not be a problem. Corruption was not at the top of my mind - getting away from the situation was. He fearlessly explained to me - how I could put some dollars in the passport, stand in the queue again and he would do the needful. I did what he said, after some hard bargaining. I was relieved to have successfully managed the situation.

I thought I escaped through the ordeal but a more audacious incident happened. One of the police guards came near me and told me that the chief of the police at the airport had asked for me. He said I was seen handing over money to the custom officer which was an offence and I could be booked for that. I could see stars by then. I never expected the travel to be so eventful from the airport. Before I could express my worry and think of way out - he too had a solution. He asked for some money, he would resolve this at his level and I need not go to the senior police. Now I could unravel the entire chain - it was a perfect co-ordination among those corrupt officials at the airport. I was wiser after the incident. Corruption is something we are used to in different spheres in Indian society. Things have changed since then or maybe I have become smarter and wiser for them to try any misadventures.

I transited via Addis Ababa, I was told that the custom officials there are not very kind and look for avenues for money. This international travel was appearing to be an exercise in handling corruption. Luckily, they did not ask for any money, even though they did look intimidating. I reached Accra in the evening. One of my colleague was waiting there to receive me. The airport was small but seemed fine. I was happy to see a well- conditioned brand new Honda car, nice well-built road till our bungalow and the big bungalow itself. I was pleasantly surprised to see some of the infrastructure like roads in very good condition; I thought they were better than Indian roads in those days. Our house was in the upscale Labone area - it was a company rented guest house at exorbitantly high rent from local standard. The house itself was big 6-bedroom duplex with big garden and courtyard. The lifestyle definitely looked like changing for better as an expat. The foreign travel sometimes do well to our living standards. In few hours my lifestyle changed from someone living in a nondescript locality in

Andheri, travelling by local trains to someone living in an upscale posh area in a capital with a large bungalow and a private car, a cook, a driver and a gardener.

The spacious bungalow in Labone - our house

When I reached the house, I remember my friends splitting the expenses of the previous night dinner. It was half a million Cedis (local currency) I think - the cost of dinner for 4 people. What - cost of a single dinner in millions? I realized I was already a millionaire with only few hundred US dollars I brought in. One dollar could fetch 5000 local currency denomination (it has stabilized since then). Soon I got used to spending in hundreds of thousands of Cedis. The currency was falling sharply and USD was a very prized currency. Dollar was welcome everywhere across the counter.

I learned that many things were imported there and hence denominated in dollars. In India, I was not used to seeing dollar as often in markets and cities. This was one of the marked differences, which I suppose had got to do with the structure of the economy. It took me quite some time to understand the state of economy there. If the country was poor, how were the roads so good? There were so many foreign cars everywhere- though many of them were second hand - but all the brands which I never saw in India. I learned my driving there on some of the finest cars and was wondering why India had huge import duties on foreign cars/second hand cars. Those were still the early days of India's economic liberalization post 1991 and foreign manufactured items were hardly available in India.

The first thing I learned after reaching Accra was that Africans are not intimidating at all, as they may have been projected at times. Most of them came out as very gentle and respecting people. They greeted warmly and talked in a friendly manner in general. In my opinion they were quite humble. As an Indian expat, I received respectful and friendly treatment from them. The Indian community is sizable among non-African communities there. Many of them were second generation migrants from Gujarat. Most Indians were into business and were well to do from the local standards. It was not that rare to see Indians in Ghana. I never felt out of place anywhere in the professional work or in the select social gathering. I was once witness to a scene when a street beggar started talking in Hindi when he saw us. His language was quite like an 'Indian beggar' - "*Bhagwan ke nam par dede, balm (give me some money in the name of God)*." I was surprised but also happy to hear an Indian language. I think it made a perfect business sense to him to learn those few Hindi words looking at well to do charitable Indians. This definitely proved that Indians were in good numbers everywhere in Accra.

A busy roundabout in Accra in year 2000

Ghana is relatively better example among the African countries. They have a running democracy. The country is by and large quite safe for people, including the foreigners. There are petty crimes but they do not, in any way, affect the sense of overall security in the city. I remember going out at midnight multiple times for attending urgent official work. A few years later when I visited Nigeria, I realized the safety is not to be taken for granted. The two neighboring countries had a marked difference when it came to security. The beaches in Lagos were told not to be safe whereas the beaches in Accra and nearby cities were perfect for outings at any time of the day. There were some very clean beaches in and around Accra.

People did work hard there for their living. Many of them were like Indians below poverty line. Working women were quite common sight across the social strata. Some of them would tie their infants behind their back with a piece of cloth. I have not seen this prevalent elsewhere. The infants would be comfortable and the mother would have both her hands free for any physical work. It was the first time I saw lady security guards as frequently being employed as men. The concept of arranged marriage in India was quite surprising to them (as it is to most of the non-indians). They believed in spending some time together before deciding on marriage. On the idea of arranged marriage one of my African colleagues had remarked "How can you buy a cat if it is still in the bag"? In Ghana the population is predominantly Christian and they have similar traditions.

My work was less stressful there, I recall. It was the first international trips for me and I did not fully understand the software I was expected to explain to the bank. Many times I would get call from the branches "Sir, good morning, the computer program is not working". Sometimes I knew the solution but many times I would not have any idea. Then a friend of mine told me a trick - "ask him to restart the server". This had twin advantages - sometimes the program started working of its own (never knew why) and it also gave more time to think at the same time. Sometimes I would use this trick multiple times with the same person. But even after 10th restart the person would very politely call, first greet and explain the same problem. Imagine something like that in India and we could get the dressing down in the first call itself, forget any greetings.

One thing that I found remarkably different, was the observance of death rituals of the near and dear ones as a sendoff ceremony rather than a mark of sorrow and grief. I attended one such funeral where the person who had expired was buried with so much of fanfare. The dress code was obviously ethnic black dress which represented mourning. His body was embalmed and kept for 30 days after his death that was being laid to rest. The activity was preceded by fashion shows, musical programs and other functions followed by a feast for all the community members. This was quite common in the culture there, I was told that they consider the burial as a send-off farewell. When I told that in India, Hindus as per their culture do not bury but conduct cremation, they thought it was quite cruel. Something that is accepted so naturally in India was inconceivable for them. The closest reasoning for them was that India, being a country of billion plus people will run out of burial space if Hindus followed a similar tradition.

I think Africa is gifted when it comes to natural beauty. Their flora and fauna, beaches, waterfalls are good to visit for the interested people. The best thing was, they were not adulterated by huge tourist inflows for obvious reasons. The waterfalls and the jungles were very naturally dean; not due to government drive to promote tourism like in other countries but because they were less frequented unlike populous tourist places. It was quite affordable as well, our usual outings used to be to go to the countryside on weekends for long drives.

Ghana had good night life because it was safe to roam around even at night. There were many night dubs in Accra. I think it was more lively than most of the Indian metro cities in that way. They mainly played English music but at times also played some Punjabi - Bhangra kind of Indian music. They were open all night on weekends. They served the local beer and other alcoholic drinks. They had very peculiar steps for what they called, was Ghanaian dance. It was nice to watch, especially when that synched up well to the local music tunes. The language was not a problem, as English is widely spoken and understood even though the local dialects are different.

I learned how to drive a car in Ghana. We did have a driver and we were strictly prohibited from driving, but it was one of the fun things - the roads were good and traffic was better and more orderly. I was astonished at the variety of the foreign cars in the small country. In India those foreign cars were very rare occurrence those days due to high custom duties. Inddentally our driver would change cars and I had the privilege of driving many luxury cars and SUVs. I spent seven months in Accra and it was a memorable stay. I did not miss India so much - we had a cook who prepared perfect Indian food, had social circle of local Indian friends and also went to Indian temples on weekends. When I left Ghana, I only wished I could return to see the same city some years later one day. It has been more than 16 years and it is quite unlikely that I might visit the country again, but the fond memories will stay with me forever.

Nigeria

Many of my colleagues who had visited Nigeria earlier, had a fasdnating story to tell on how they were asked for money at the airport. The security people would very unassumingly ask - *"brother something for us"?* We were advised to keep the change to avoid inconvenience. At one instance when one of our friend said he did not have a change for a hundred dollars, the gun toting security personnel was willing to accompany him till the hotel to get the change. The payment to the police at the airport almost looked like their legitimate due. I am sure the things have changed for the better since 2007, when I travelled there. The security used to be the biggest concern probably. We were explicitly told not to hire public taxis even at the airport.

The day we landed in Lagos, it was marked by a sectarian conflict in Abuja in which scores of people were killed. Our client meeting started with offering a moment of mourning for them. It was surprising that such violence had been common occurrence but still received very little coverage in the international press. Nigeria is one of the largest producers of oil in the world but wealth was conspicuous by its absence in the common society. I never expected it to be a rich country like the Middle-East (thanks to the documentaries on poverty and armed conflicts on CNN), but the lack of development was quite visible everywhere. One can argue that the abundance of oil has not much helped this country's fortune. Some believe, it has rather added to the miseries of the people giving rise to the armed militia fighting with the government and rampant corruption everywhere. Whether at the checkin counters at the airport or an ordinary police check point - they appeared sometimes demanding money for no reason.

On way from airport, we passed over a long bridge ranging 11 kilometers over sea backwater. This bridge (The Third Mainland Bridge) that connected Lagos to the mainland was the longest bridge in Africa till 1996 and one of the longest in the world. I understood that it was probably one of the few testimonies to the infrastructure development that happened in 90s. Almost every house had their private generators for electricity. Nigeria can surely be an example of how natural resource alone (even something like oil) is not a necessary and sufficient condition for the countries' economic well-being. The policies created by the government had a major bearing in creating an equitable growth in society.

In both Nigeria and Ghana, what I realized in other countries in Africa too, absence of 'middle class' population can be quite notable. There were many wealthy people, who had fancy cars and houses and there were other extremes who would be largely deprived and poor. Too much of wealth can create a sense of entitlement (especially if it is in overall environment of poverty); at the same time complete lack of it can make one resigned to their destiny and follow the beaten path. A middle class fills in the gap well- they have just enough resources to struggle in society and change the course of their own destiny. They have basic education and willingness to work hard to improve their lifestyles. In my view they have played a very key role in the economic development of a country like India and now hold the key to future promises. The Indian economic journey is all about millions of upwardly moving middle class. For them, the dream of upliftment is tough but achievable - it makes the struggle worth it. There are enough success stories for them for this struggle not being a blind chase. They form the most dynamic and industrious component of the society and hold key to the future economic growth. I am not sure why such a layer of the society could not build up in Africa like India. Equitable growth is a subject of in-depth study in any society including India, but I can surely say the situation is much worse in Africa. Coming back to the Government policies, they play the most important part in establishing a framework (whether education, tax cuts or social measures) that leads to the overall well-being and an equitable society.

Like many other African countries, Indians have migrated to Nigeria and consist of a very dominant business community. I saw some of the Indian bikes and automobiles among many others. There were few showrooms of Indian auto manufacturers. Indian bikes were quite common. Crazy all direction traffic at many places, reminded me of Indian roads. The random moving vehicles were left to fend for themselves to find the best alternatives to maneuver on the roads. The roads themselves were not as good as what I saw in Ghana. One of my friends quipped to compare Ghana and Nigeria - if Nigeria were India, Ghana would be Singapore. Now having visited all these places I could relate to what he meant but not sure how accurate it would be.

I also found another interesting concept there called 'Okada - motor cycle taxis' - these are the bikers who ferry passengers as the pillion riders. They were quite commonly used by the local populace, even to ferry light goods by the small shopkeepers. This was an example of the out-of-the-box innovation probably. The Okada was cheap, fast, timely and very appropriate for the messy traffic. I understand this 'Okada' like service is also popular in few other African countries like Kenya.

The other thing that was noticeable there, was the range of things that was being sold on the roads in the middle of the busy traffic. It looked to me there was quite a bit of retail industry there on those roads. They would sell practically everything- coffee machines, SIM card, clothes, food item and toys. It was difficult to believe how people completed their transaction including bargaining for all such items - may be the slow moving traffic at places was the reason. Sights of the hawkers selling small and big items maneuvering the moving vehicles in the scorching sun were not the best of the sights for the tourists. Public transport was mainly in the form of Yellow colored small buses that were always packed to the brim. I did not see anything like public taxi in the traditional way as one would find in any other country. Either there were new and old cars or these yellow matadors kind of transport.

I sensed that in Africa the natives did not get all that they possibly rightfully deserved. The prosperity had been denied to them possibly due to inadequate policies of the governments earlier and now the multi-national companies that were just siphoning out all the wealth. There was not much growth of the local industries. The globalization too had not helped them much because they were ill prepared for it. They had not been able to build the critical mass of human capital that could have helped them to latch on the globalization bandwagon to their benefit. For the uninitiated, globalization can further strip them of the opportunities. If one has to compare that with India, one can argue that the protected policies of the government were not necessarily bad. Now that there is a sizeable mass (population, industry, technology) and a proven methodology like outsourcing in India - globalization is a liberator rather than a threat. Many countries in Africa have missed the preparation phase for this global competition. On top of this they have been mired in internal conflicts to make matter worse. In spite of some of them having good natural resources - like oil, gold or diamonds, it has not necessarily helped their country's economic well-being.

For many of us who visited Nigeria for a brief period, the only concern was security and safety. There were horror stories of how common it was to encounter looters in the middle of the city who would demand money and turn violent if their demands were not met. There were instances when people were robbed off of even the dothes that they were wearing. Even the hotels were not safe and the robbers would sneak in at times. Many area were no go after evening. Most advisable way of commuting was in the company provided taxis with adequate safety arrangements; sometimes they would use blue beacons.

I recall the day we were supposed to catch our flight back from Lagos. Our local partner who was helping us with the logistics, asked for the taxi well 4 hours earlier. When I asked him why 4 hours, his response was, one hour delay was accounted for the taxi driver himself to report. He was right, the taxi driver did not turn up in time at all. In fact the driver came more than an hour late. We lost hope that we would be able to catch the flight. Looking at the traffic that was slow moving at several places, I thought it would take us a long time. Suddenly we saw a series of cars with flashing beacons on top going past us. Our driver said, it was the cavalcade of some important minister. He had an idea already, if he followed the cavalcade, we could reach in time. The traffic was cleared up for the cavalcade and to our good fortune, we reached the airport in time and left Lagos.

Egypt

In my opinion, Egypt shared with Africa only a place in the map because in many ways it was more like Middle East country than Africa. It is an Islamic country but looked quite modern those days. One of reasons could be because it has been a tourism based country. When I landed at the Cairo airport sometime in 2001 - I saw many agents looking for the tourists. It was somewhat like when people come out at Indian airports at Mumbai or Delhi and the taxi drivers followed them persistently. I was told that they were reliable in Cairo - so followed one of them. He took me to a nearby small shop and offered different tour packages for the period. Within minutes everything was fixed and he asked me for an advance and provided a receipt for the same. I handed the advance and hoped that he did not cheat me and pick me up from the hotel the other day. He did come promptly as promised. I later learned that these travel agents never duped the tourists and were closely monitored by the government. Because of the Islamic laws and special focus on tourism the petty crimes were quite less. Whatever the reason, I found the whole tourism infrastructure was well developed in Cairo and was quite conducive to the foreign travelers.

As I travelled to different tourist places in Cairo - I remembered the history lessons on Mesopotamia being one of the oldest civilizations. A lot of it looked like India - the streets, people, everything. I was told that an Indian can easily pass for an Egyptian. When I was passing through one of the souvenir markets my guide commented that this was similar to a market in some old Indian cities like Varanasi. I could guess that because the setup was quite similar to a typical Indian market where people bargained to buy local handicrafts. There were not many tourists from India though as there were from Japan or Europe. I doubted if there would be any significant Indian population there.

Excavated area near Giza Pyramids

The river Nile is revered by the people of Egypt. The civilization owes a lot to it since its inception. It is respected somewhat like the Ganges in India, possibly even more. As I went through the streets and the local guide explained each monument and landmark - one can easily start wondering about the human life, thousands of years back. How they evolved through the ages? The history comes alive there; the textbook narration about the human existence thousands of years back looked much more real. There are wonders like the Pyramids - that can keep people thinking how they were created some four thousand years back. The size of each stone, the geometry, architecture of the Pyramid and the safe tunnel leading to the bottom where the mummies were kept - even with current technical knowhow is a matter of speculation. The paintings on the wall speak about the richness of the culture and how people thought about themselves and the environment. Some of those beliefs have not changed even now - particularly the way people see themselves viz. a viz. nature. I think various religions carry a good amount of those elements and only the scientific link from those culture seems missing. Looking at the marvel of the architecture of the Pyramids and storage of mummies - it can be a subject of debate as to which period was scientifically more advanced. They conducted a laser show called light and music show' on the backdrop of the pyramids where the story goes back to the known threads about some of the kings and their sons. The national museum contains many mummies that are preserved and put on display for the tourists. They look real - but the year tag near them like 4000 years back seems too unreal. The ancient history comes alive in those museums there - it no longer remains some amalgamation of dates with incidents which are difficult to remember.

Egypt is an Islamic country but I did not see much perceptible difference as such. When I was traveling by the car the guide showed many women who were driving cars. His view of life in Cairo was quite progressive in many ways. He waved at one of the woman who was travelling by our side and she waved back with a smile too. Looking at the people in the street it did seem that things were different there from other Islamic nations. Later we went to one of the oldest mosque and I put the same question whether women were allowed inside the pious place of worship. He went at length to explain to me the deeper philosophy around the same. I am not sure if I followed all that - all I could conclude was they were not allowed for some religious reasons and the women were fine with that.

River cruise on the Nile is one of the main attractions of Cairo. It takes a couple of hours along the river. It provides a night view of the city. They organize dinner on the way and Arabic music is accompanied by a performance by belly dancers. At the end of the trip they also provide a printed photograph of each visitor with the belly dancer which makes one wonder when did she come so close to be seen in the same photo frame. Those were the days when cellphones were still not that common and selfies were yet to be discovered. Most camera still used the rolls, so a printed photograph was a good souvenir to get from those Nile cruises. I also saw people arranging wedding parties on some of the cruises. I thought the tourism infrastructure in Cairo was quite evolved. The sense of safety, active monitoring by the government and the existence of great historic monuments made it one of the excellent tourist destinations. If one compares the tourism potential of India and Egypt, it is very much similar. However, there are clear differences too. Historically interesting monuments are spread across multiple regions in India. That is a challenge, because a quick 3-4 days concentrated tourism package will not make any sense in India. The tourism industry in Cairo was definitely more structured and it contributed significantly to their GDP. I was told it was one of the reasons that Egyptian Pound was so strong.

I visited Cairo again ten years later sometime in 2009. By then I had visited many other countries and was better equipped to do a realistic comparison with other big cities of the world. Cairo is one of the largest cities of the world and the only large city in Egypt where more than one fifth of the country's population lived. When I landed at the airport this time, I realized it had not changed much since my last visit. It was the same old small and crowded airport which was there earlier - I could easily compare it to the small and crowded airports that some of Indian cities were having few years back. Last few years all these airports in India had improved for better but Cairo helped me remember those bad old days. There was all-new terminal ready for use and it looked big and modern. This was still a late catch-up, considering the fact that Egypt was primarily dependent on tourism and airports were the most visible component. All the south-east Asian countries had built world class airports precisely for that reason.

Tunnel way to Mummy storage inside the Pyramid

Once inside the city, I could remember some of the landmarks especially in the older part of the city. Not much had changed there, only more buildings had turned greyer. I wondered whether all these buildings were constructed in grey or dust color. I was told that they did have some color like yellow or green but years of pollution and neglect have left most of the buildings of the same color. The local Egyptian partner said that many of these buildings were similar to the old structures in Mumbai. Understandably most of the developments had happened in the other side of the city and the older parts were left out. The landmarks near the Nile like the tall Sheraton building, the cylindrical tower immediately helped me recollect the image of Cairo that I had from my earlier visit.

The traffic in the city was as chaotic as we are used to seeing in any busy city in India. Honking, sporadic lane change, people crossing roads, all were as unsystematic as it could get. Half of the cars showed dents of small and big accidents. Some of the cars on the road were so old (especially the black taxis) and so many times banged that the few new car owners would be scared to even get near them. For some taxis, I guess the only requirement was to have four wheels and an engine. For some cars, the front and back lights were broken, windows cracked and the body paints long gone-off. Once, while travelling in a taxi I wanted to bring down the glass window as it was very hot. I found there was nothing like a door handle, it was broken - the driver promptly gave me the broken handle and told me how to use it - it was quite funny.

Negotiating for the street taxi was an art. I did not find any taxi had any meter for charges. The negotiation depended on a lot of things like one being a foreigner, the place of pick up etc. I was surprised to know that a taxi from my hotel to a particular place would cost me something which is double than what my other colleagues were paying for a distance which was double than mine. So if the place of pickup or drop is a good hotel the charges could be double. If one does not talk the local language there was a certain premium to be paid for that. I was told that the taxi guys understood little English to quote the charges well enough but they would use the ignorance to their advantage. Anyway this was no worry for people like us who were used to such fleecing by the taxi drivers in India. But as one of my friend living there said - these people may fleece you for a bit of money but would never get into heated argument with you. Even when they were negotiating they were friendlier than trying to force their way. The city was largely very safe unlike other crime infested large cities.

For as far as I could see, this city was dosest to Tehran in many aspects like people, culture, look of the building, traffic everything. It looked slightly more modern if one has to guess by the outlets of McDonalds, KFCs and other American brands. There were few big malls that had come up since my last visit 10 years back. Not that all were happy with this perceived influence of American culture. I was chatting with our Egyptian business partner and his view was that one of the reasons that the sodety was falling apart, was the influence of the American media and blind following of the same with complete disregard to the local culture and the history of Egypt. It was a common problem in Egypt that people went to Europe and US for better education and never returned. Some of these problems sounded familiar to me - the brain drain phenomenon in India. The other impact he felt of this media deluge was shortened attention span. This living for the moment, he believed was a media created phenomenon, primary driven by the American consumerism which never had any depth or serious thinking around it.

I wanted to repeat some of the tourist spots that I had been in my last trip to re-live some of those experiences. A Nile cruise and visit to Pyramid were surely among them. This time we took a boat though - the sailing boat. We were three of us as we settled for a small boat after a good round of negotiation. We bought bottles of beer and for next one hour it was a nice cruise in the water getting different views of the city. Unlike the last time it did not have a big ship with belly dandng and food on-board, but this was equally enjoyable. Sometimes the patrolling police would come near to our boat and the boatman would tell us to hide the beer bottles, he would manage the police. It was just another reason for him to daim the extra tip. I thought he deserved more - these people were extremely polite and friendly even while negotiating hard for money. The city was very busy all the time, even during late in the night. This was a good weather season and I understood that people spend lot of time out in the city in late evenings and nights. It was not unusual to see traffic jams even late nights.

Pyramids were the next on my agenda to visit. That was one thing I did not expect to be any different from the last visit; after all they have been like this since last four thousand years. So after a long and strenuous traffic I reached the Pyramid site. This time I was alone and just wanted to spend some time there rather than buying the tour packages. The moment I took a ticket and entered the premises there were few people who started insisting on taking a guide and a tonga ride. For as much as I tried, I could not get rid of them. I was finally forced to take a tonga for a ride which I never thought was worth it, since I had been through all that earlier. This time I was less awestruck by the structure. I noticed things other than the structure such as the place being such a great piece of human achievement was unkempt and could have been organized much better. Having seen other places of historical importance so well maintained in Europe this monument certainly deserved more respect. The tonga tour consisted of two different tours; the first part was the pyramid and Sphinx and the other part was passing through the residences which looked like slums to me. It must have been carefully designed keeping in mind western tourists who would be equally intrigued with the local way of living. The tonga trip was less of the Pyramid - we stopped in between for the horse to drink water, buy some grass etc. for what seemed to me an unusually long trip outside the pyramids.

On way back to airport I could see that the newer part of the city had come up well as it looked more structured with new modern buildings around. Like many large cities in India, Cairo too was changing very fast. There was a large hardworking population making their way upwards - it looked similar to India in many sense. The people there too showed lot of warmth towards Indians. The immigrant Indians had still not found favorite with Cairo - may be because they didn't think there was much difference between Mumbai and Cairo.

I think language could be one of the main reasons too. Had Egypt been English speaking as much as India, the so called outsourcing boom must have benefitted it as much. This country was not as much fortunate to have easy money from oil like the Arab countries.

Though the country looked quite open and progressive politically, it did look like something was amiss. Those were the last few years of President Hosni Mubarak, of his 30 years long rule in Egypt. I thought most Egyptians considered him a benevolent authoritarian. The country was pretty stable compared to what has followed since then, particularly now discredited Arab Spring. The so-called revolution characterized by long demonstrations in Tahrir Square has created more uncertainty in a country which was illustrious land of pharaohs at some point in history.

Mauritius

Mauritius, to some extent is a beautiful amalgamation of African, Indian and European cultures. It has a large population of Indian origin that came to Mauritius as indentured labors and slaves some 150 years back, primarily to work in the sugar factories and construction. I visited *Apravasi Ghat* in Port Louis - it is a historical place in the capital where these indentured labors were first received. It is a heritage site now. Though it depicts a dark past, today's Mauritius is one the most developed countries in Africa. Over the years these people have worked hard and created wealth for themselves and the country. It was a French colony some point in time, and that impact was evident in the local language called Creole. A small fraction of the population do speak Bhojpuri with a very unique French accent. Some of the folk songs that they used to sing during their cultural festivals, were in Bhojpuri. The country is very systematic and structured, very much like a small European country. The cost of living is relatively high.

33m tall statue ofMangal Mahadev (Shiva Statue)
at Ganga Talao

One of the most remarkable things that I noticed was, even though Indians migrated there very long time back, they have carried on with their cultural traditions. Hinduism is the majority religion in Mauritius. The country celebrates many of the Hindu festivals, there are temples all around. One such place that I visited was Ganga Talao. It is one of the most sacred pilgrimage place for Hindus in Mauritius. The folklore is that the sacred water from Ganges was mixed with this lake to make it as pious as Ganga. It has a gigantic statue of Lord Shiva which looks amazing. When I went there, it was partly clouded so we could not clearly see the top part of the statue. During Mahashivratri, the devotees leave their home barefoot for Ganga Talao and carry water to offer to Lord Shiva. A similar tradition of offering prayers is prevalent in many parts of India but I was surprised to hear this ritual being practiced every year with lot of devotion in a far off place like Mauritius. Many of the Indian restaurants there would play melodious old Hindi songs of Bollywood. We generally don't hear those songs in India anymore. It looked like their memory with their home country was still intact through those songs, though several decades have passed by. Sometimes we read that some of those Indian descendants travel to India to trace back their roots more than a hundred years ago.

Mauritius is a country of beautiful beaches, sun and sand. It is one of the most favored holiday destinations, away from the hustle and bustle of the big cities. For those of us who like water sports like scuba diving, skiing, sea bed walking there can't be a better place than Mauritius. Renting a car and going on long drive over

A clear day view from my apartment in Mauritius

the weekend was another good experience. The roads were good and the country is pretty safe. Once one of my colleagues who lived there, commented that the crime rate was low there because the place was too small for the thieves to hide. Even if they stole a car, it was almost sure they would be caught within a few hours unless they dumped it in the sea.

I used to travel to Mauritius on a frequent basis for work. Probably I was one of the rare ones who would go to Mauritius for business. Most of the times, newlyweds choose this place as their honeymoon destination. It is one of the few countries that allow on-arrival visa for Indians. I remember my travel to office from the hotel included a boat ride every day which was so refreshing. The work life in general was quite laid back - somewhat like in a small European country. Party on the yachts and big boats were very common sight. People used to go for long cruises. It had all the ingredients for a great holiday experience amidst the most natural setup of beautiful beaches.

Port Louis - ships and cruises

The island is still quite pristine and less polluted unlike other big cities. At some point in time not too far, Mauritius was uninhabited and was full of unique spedes of plants and birds. Many of them, it is believed became extinct once the human settlements started. One such legendary story is that of 'Dodo bird'. Before the Dutch sailors started frequenting the island, these birds were in abundance. These were unique birds, large in size that did not fly and survived on island vegetation. These birds were easy prey for the sailors for their food. As the settlers came in, the dodo birds started diminishing and finally became extinct in 1662. The settlers also brought in other animals and rodents that killed these birds. This extinction of dodo bird is largely a case study of how human settlements have at times created the ecological imbalance. The dodo birds are part of many local folklores for their unique appearance, inability to fly and not being able to defend themselves from being preyed on.

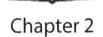

Chapter 2

Middle-East, some little travelled destinations

Iran

I was quite looking forward to my visit to Tehran. I am sure it is not among the widely visited cities in the current context and will categorize as an exotic destination today. We hear so much (not necessarily very positive) about it in media, so visiting the city and having a firsthand experience was quite exdting.

Lot of myths were broken for me when I visited Tehran. The first one was, I thought the weather in Tehran would be hot - it must be sweltering desert like other middle-east countries. It turned out be a hilly city where the temperature goes subzero and it snows in the winter. The airport was fairly small and crowded from the international standards. I heard that a new airport had been built but was so far from the main city that it was highly inconvenient. This was sometime way back in 2005.

One of the notices that caught my attention at the airport was the one that requested *"All women whether foreign or Iranian must cover their heads"*. This reminded me that I was in an Islamic country which followed Islamic guidelines more than others. In the city and everywhere, I saw women covered usually as per the traditional Islamic dresses. Some of the parks in the city, I did see the couples walking hand in hand but that was not that common. The discussion with some of the people suggested that it was a growing trend among the younger generations who were more open to changing times. I remember one incident - once I was dicking the photograph of one of my friends. In the background, inadvertently I captured the image of a girl who was working in the same office. Incidentally she had not covered her head (as some of them don't if not in public places) which was captured in the photograph. When she got to know about the photograph, she objected strongly. I was scared when she almost broke into tears and insisted to delete the photograph till I did. She was afraid that her photograph without her head covered could land her in trouble. In the work places, especially like banks, there were a good number of working women.

Anti-Americanism was in the air everywhere in Iran in 2005. When I was going for a business meeting, I was told that wearing a tie there was considered to be a symbol of Americanism and hence not acceptable. A business formal there meant a suite or blazer without a tie. The business meeting started with a brief prayer everyday - that was an unfamiliar beginning of day for me. There were no Me Donald's or Burger Ring or any such American food chain - but I was quite surprised that they had almost all copy outlets and the concepts sans the American brand names. So, I found a drink which would taste and look like Pepsi or Coke but it would be a different local label. Most of the American companies were banned to operate in Iran due to prevailing sanctions that time, but the local business had developed an alternative or had developed a way to get around the bans. It must have been quite frustrating for their business environment. The ban had not helped the prosperity and the growth of otherwise such a beautiful city and country. People though, had learned innovative ways to live with restrictions. Alcohol was banned in the restaurants but I was told that many people brewed it at their home. 'Prostitution' was banned but people could get into marriages for as short as 15 days after which the marriage would be void.

Shah's Palace in Tehran - A museum now

During our conversation with colleagues there, it was hard to skip the subject of Islamic revolution and the impact it had on everything, including their way of lives. I went to see the Shah's palace which was converted into the public museum. Mohammed Reza Shah ruled the country as an autocrat with active support from Americans. It was culturally closer to west that time. I once watched a TV program on Islamic revolution - one of the images I remember very vividly, was the New Year celebration when Shah had invited Jimmy Carter over drinks which were beamed across in the Iranian population. This showed how distant Shah had travelled from the reality. The monarch was celebrating New Year in a conservative Islamic country and drinking alcohol in full public view. This was just a few days before his palace was stormed and the Shah fled out of Iran. The populist move overthrew all the semblance of Americanism and converted the country into an Islamic theocracy. Shah's objective had been to align Iran with the west. I understood that Tehran was a good western tourist destination and had a happening night life before the Islamic revolution. All such semblances of the western civilization were gone after the revolution. The subsequent theocratic government not only asserted its Islamic identity but also turned out be a big opposing nation for the west and US in particular.

As an Indian, I did not find out-of-place for the few weeks I was there. In fact, there was quite perceptible warmth towards Indians in general. Some people seemed to have visited and studied in India as well. This was possibly due to the historically good relations between the two countries. Even culturally, I think India is closer to Iran - the mosques, structures, people's hospitability - all looked quite familiar to the Asian value system. In their local language Farsi, there were some common words in Sanskrit and Hindi. I recall our business presentations in Tehran. An English translator was hard to find. The best we could find was a local partner, who spoke good English but was a veterinary doctor by profession. He would translate every sentence after I spoke and he would take at least thrice as much time and lot more sentences to explain. After sometime, I got suspicious if he was only translating what I was saying or adding his own story. There was no way to ascertain for me though. May be, it was as tough for him to explain banking terms being a veterinary doctor. Every time he brought a book of English dictionary for our presentations and meetings. He would refer to them during meetings as well.

Casual view on a wad in Tehran

I was perfectly at ease with the traffic there - there were cars moving in all directions without much regard to the traffic rules. Like Indian traffic, it was based on 'drive wherever the space is'. I remember once we missed a turn by more than a kilometer, the driver did not take a U- turn; instead he drove back in the reverse gear for the entire distance. Though it was late in the evening for such adventure, the taxi driver was candid in saying that he had done it quite often. There were cars all around - the oil being one of the cheapest commodities there. Crossing the road could be a small project for unfamiliar people.

They took pride in hospitality of people and considered it as their core values. This was akin to the Indian value system. One of the nights, I visited the 'hill palace' which was an excellent place where people would go for an outing and have dinners etc. It must have been a great tourist destination at some time. The food was also quite familiar with things like Kebabs and Olives among many other things. People in general were surely not happy about the image that was projected in the western media. Most of the times we do not realize that the world knows these countries from the lens of the western media which is not very kind to them.

I am sure a city like Tehran will evoke multiple thoughts for many. There can be conflicting observations as a political entity, economic isolation, rich cultural heritage, Islamic values, warm and receptive people, but people at large definitely deserved better bargain from the world in general. If one can discount the general image projected, as Iranians they were as nice human beings as anywhere else in the world. Some people rued the lost standing in the international projection post the Islamic revolution.

Kuwait

Whenever I remember my travel to Kuwait, the key takeaway was the prosperity that oil can bring to a nation without having industrious native population. The abundant natural resource like oil can itself make a country prosperous. One just needed to be lucky enough to be born in these countries. If there could be any class disparity in a society, it could not be more evident than in Kuwait. There is an immigrant working population, mainly from the Asian countries at one end of the spectrum and the resident Sheikhs at the other end of the spectrum. There is hardly any other class in between. This is similar to the other typical oil rich countries in middle-east. The immigrant working population works hard for their employers. This division is visible everywhere in the public life from the airports to the shopping malls to the public transport.

We went to a famous shopping mall on one of the evenings. It was quite modern and was filled with all international brands. Things were very costly by our standards but that did not deter the rich Kuwaitis from buying them. Thanks to the oil money, Kuwaiti currency Dinar was one of strongest currency with 1 dinar being almost equal to 3 US dollar. The approach of the shopkeepers towards the prospective customers was quite notable - they would clearly identify and attend to traditionally dressed Kuwaitis who they knew could afford to spend. For rest of us it really took lot of effort, even to get their serious attention. Based on their previous experience, they must have a justifiable reason for preferential customer treatments. There were Indians and other Asians in Kuwait but most of them were menial labor or the blue collar workers. For them these shops were merely for looking. We would also see occasionally the local Kuwaitis with his burka clad wife (sometimes wives) buying numerous things in those shops. They would have Asian maids taking care of their kids while their women spent times in shopping.

City view from Kuwait Tower

One has to be careful while taking photographs at the public places because sometime it may inadvertently land them in trouble. I recall an incident in a prominent shopping mall when we were taking photographs with our friends. We saw one Sheikh talking animatedly in Arabic and moving towards us. He looked angry as he moved towards us. We got scared but we struggled to find why he was upset. Later we understood that he suspected us of capturing their (and family) image in the background. I had not seen a photography restricted areas in places like shopping malls in other countries. We were able to convince him of our intentions and even deleted the photograph. I was, since then very circumspect while taking photographs in the public places, especially where there could be sheikhs with their families.

The weather was sweltering hot for the pedestrians. It was very uncomfortable for walking along the streets during the day. For public transport, there were good air-conditioned mini buses. For experience, I once travelled in one of these buses. The astonishing part was almost all the passengers were Asian, predominantly Indian. The sight inside the bus was not very different from a crowded bus in Delhi. To make the environment more familiar they played Bollywood songs too. Those buses looked like mini-India by themselves. I doubt if one could ever find any Kuwaitis in those public buses. The local Kuwaitis would have swanky cars and would never be seen in any public transport (I could recognize only from their traditional Arabic dresses). The police vans were all BMW cars - it was a big surprise for me in 2006. Even in many developed countries police were not that indulgent. Comparing that with the rugged Jeeps that the police had in India, this was a luxury to expect for a government agency. The government has surplus oil money and they rightfully use it to the benefit of their citizens.

While discussing with some of the colleagues, I understood that even the policies of business were quite benign to the local Kuwaiti citizens e.g. a business venture needed to have a Kuwaiti as a partner. This Kuwaiti partner would not be obliged to work as hard but facilitate adherence to local rules; in the end they would share half of the profits. These rules ensured that the citizens always got share in the business growth along with the non-Kuwaiti partners. The country always indulged the local citizen and the huge oil wealth had made it possible economically. Their expenses like education, medical and few other things were taken care of. I wondered they would have very few things to worry about in life. The common joke there was that each Kuwaiti had an oil pump in his backyard and every time he needed some money all that he had to do was just to pump few barrels. A typical proud Kuwaiti, I was told, will never bend to pick up his purse in public, even if it falls- he would rather let it go and pass by. Kuwaitis are born rich and are proud of their richness. When I think of the overvalued dinars, only a Kuwaitis with so much of wealth could afford to do that.

Kuwait had a large expat population from western countries as well who worked in the white collar jobs, unlike Asians. Due to the exposure to western lifestyles, this country is fairly modern and people in general are quite open. In spite of Kuwait being an Islamic country, women could be seen in modern western dresses in the offices. It was still more open and tolerant to foreign culture and values. I was told that eating in public during Ramadan fasting days was not acceptable there. This was something everyone had to abide. I had to be extra cautious not to pick up anything to eat or drink when I was walking through some of the shops. At least, I had to strongly resist the temptation to drink something due to the hot weather.

A country like Kuwait triggers a thought on relative comparison of inherited wealth vs acquired wealth. Most people around the world work hard to acquire prosperity but when one inherits a good fortune already, I am not sure what one's motivation in life would be. Too much of inherited wealth can make the life boring also, as most of our work life is directed towards economic objectives. In India, for an average man the job is cut out for him since the day he is born. It starts with competition in education, then getting a good job then stability and career growth and so on. For those who are born with silver spoons, the circumstances do not force them to acquire good education or skills. Due to these factors I don't think the native Kuwaitis are as industrious or entrepreneurial as they could be. They don't exert for many things. They rather get people from Asian countries to work for them. The immigration policies were quite timed for the same.

The immigrants work for the natives and do not enjoy anywhere near the kind of benefits and lifestyles that their employers did. If one does not believe in wealth by birth but in acquiring it by personal work, industry, skill and talent, he or she can get frustrated by seeing the dichotomy in native and immigrant population's lifestyles in Kuwait.

Flight back from Kuwait to India was no different from a crowded bus in India. I was booked in an Air India flight which incidentally continues to be one of the worst airlines even today. All passengers (mostly blue collar workers from these countries) would carry large bags, so much so that the hand baggage cabin would be packed to the brim. Additionally, they would carry separately, many duty free liquor bottles. The boarding process used to be very noisy. I would not have been surprised if the flight announcement had said *"beware of the pick pockets on this flight, they may be sitting next to you"*. During the flight, many of these passengers would avail all possible drinks. I remember, how once my co-passenger kept requesting for more and more drinks and he would not stop. After sometime the air hostess called the well-built male crew who shouted at the flier - *"this is not a bar, stop asking for more drinks"*. I wondered if he worked as bouncer in some pub earlier. At the same time, I always wondered if there was a more respectful way of dealing with such passengers in these flights.

United Arab Emirates

When I travelled to Abu Dhabi, I was told by the visa agent to wear a formal suit while passing through the immigration. I never understood the logic behind this until I landed there. This was sometime in 2012, when UAE was still very common destination for the South

Asians going in search of blue collar work in construction industry or domestic helps. The scene at the immigration point was nothing short of chaos, as many of them would travel abroad for the first time and would not be aware of travel procedures. They would also be illiterate at times. The immigration queue was long for them and there were extra procedures like retina scan etc. Very few Indians go there for white collar work. Hence wearing a business suit at least helped during the immigration clearance. It was a weird advice, but quite useful.

I had travelled there during the Ramadan times. It was a fasting period for majority of the population there. It was improper to be seen eating in public, though it was not strictly banned. My memories include eating chocolates in closed corner of the office premises or even the washroom at times. I think it is also a psychological effect that when we are told that we can't eat as often during the day, we feel hungrier. It was difficult time in that sense. The food items could be home delivered during lunch but the restaurants were closed mandatorily. The dinner during these fasting days were something that people would really relish, especially the meat lovers. I was invited for some of those dinners and was surprised at the number of food items and delicacies. Arabian food has lot of similarity with Indian food.

This was one more country where the oil reserves have created huge wealth without any need for the native citizens to work hard. Just like in Kuwait the society looked clearly segregated with rich Emiratis at one end and blue collar construction workers on the other end of the spectrum. Last few years, many technology professionals have also moved there. The IT workplace was entirely filled by Indians. In fact in the offices there, one would forget if it was a typical Indian IT work center of Bangalore. The native Emiratis were least engaged in the business activities which were managed by the immigrants. Some cases the government policies stipulated that certain business positions could only be held by Emiratis. I recall one such appointment of a local Emirati as IT project manager in the bank. He had been transferred from the passport department where he had been doing visa stamping thus far. This was the height of multi-skilling (or possibly the lack of it). I wondered how a visa stamper could be an IT manager the very next day without any background or training. Later, I understood he was only supposed to be a titular head. In all probability, he would never even visit the IT department. There would be a real IT project manager who would shadow this person and do the real work. When I met this ghost IT project manager once, he had no expectation from his Emirati counterpart. This was too much of a luxury at work and only an oil rich country like UAE could afford it.

Abu Dhabi looked like any modern city with new multi storied buildings and glass structures. The infrastructure like roads were one of the best. Though UAE is an Islamic country, it did look like any other normal Asian setup. It did not have the fear of religious police as in Saudi Arabia who secretly kept a watch on people at public places. Here the social life was closer to Dubai which is the trading hub and one of the most modern cities in the world. During the period that I stayed, the weather was extremely hot, making it very inconvenient for any tourism, especially open area ones. To protect from the hot weather there would be air-conditioning everywhere. However, it was also very common sight where the construction workers would be working under strong heat without much amenities. There had been many reports of exploitation of these workers by the local contractors. The extreme working condition of poor at one end while the opulent wealth on the other end was quite evident. I don't think they ever had a concept of middle dass like India who could improve their educational, economic and social position by hard work and entrepreneurship. The class divide was more stark and rigid. Thanks to their immense oil wealth they could always attract immigrants to do odd jobs for them. With recent slowdown in the oil based economies, it would be interesting to see these countries re-discover themselves and adapt to the new realities. Even the attractiveness of these countries for the blue collar workers have come down with slowing down of construction work. Even the Emiratis are now willing to work for their living, at least in big shops and businesses.

Every day while going to the office from hotel we used to pass by Etihad towers, one of the marvels in construction. It is a series of 5 tall towers which adorn the blue sky. All towers are more than 200 meters tall and are very artistically designed with beautiful curvature. I could somewhat compare it to the Suntec towers in Singapore. It looked like a similar concept. The Etihad towers, however are quite modern and artistic. The towers shine with the beautiful glass and steel structure.

One of the greatest attraction in Abu Dhabi is the desert safari. There were tour packages arranged from the hotel. They take the travelers to the desert where the car ride itself is very adventurous. It would be followed up by a camel ride and entertainment programs like belly dancing. Some of my friends who had seen such safaris strongly recommended to take the opportunity. I was skeptical, primarily because of the Ramadan season and strong heat. I was told during this period the entertainment programs were curtailed and food and drinks were restricted as well. I also thought it may not be a good idea to stay out and feel thirsty or hungry during the festival time. Eventually, I decided not to go for it. I still don't know whether it was a good idea because I have never ever been to a desert safari. It is also less likely that I will travel to Abu Dhabi again. Sometimes it is good to go with the conventional wisdom and visit as many places especially when in a foreign country.

Turkey

I have travelled to Turkey multiple times but the first trip was more adventurous than the later ones. It was the initial days of swine flu when it was spreading very fast and reports of many people dying in Mexico were doing rounds. During my flight from Copenhagen to Istanbul, we saw few flight attendants wearing masks and taking temperature of one person periodically. One can imagine how scary it could be especially during the early days when very little was known about it other than the obsessive fear and scare. Everyone in the flight was showing signs of worry and for the people sitting next to the patient, it was a really panicking situation. The worst thing in these situations is, no one can do anything but hope that the suspect was not suffering from the dreaded flu. To the dismay of everyone, there was an announcement in the flight that one of the passengers was showing the sign of Swine Influenza and the crew members would distribute face masks and gloves. They distributed the same and after that it was a bizarre sight where everyone was wearing a mask and gloves and carefully managing to eat food in very awkward way. Some skipped the food for this fear of exposing themselves to the virus. This was the new danger in air travel possibly, no one could have imagined such problems earlier. Later on, when I told it to my colleagues in Istanbul - they were so scared that they relieved me of my part of the work in the meeting.

Istanbul earlier known as Constantinople is a historic city and one of the largest in the world. Attracted by this beautiful city, Napoleon had once said that "If earth were a single state Constantinople would have been its capital". It was a busy city and had been witness to great historic events from the times of Romans and even before. It was the capital of East Roman empire known as Byzantine. It has survived many wars and conflicts. The final lasting acquisition was from Ottoman Turks who were the mighty empire which began in 1453 and lasted till the last century before Turkey was declared a republic in 1923. Mustafa Kemal Ataturk is supposed to be the architect of modern Turkey. The city was full of the historical monuments and structures and could be of great interest to the historians.

The beautiful Ayasofya mosque

For those taking interest in the evolution of religion, Istanbul could be a subject of much deeper studies. It was a prominent center of Orthodox Christianity during the Roman Empire. It has one of oldest and most famous churches of that era. With the arrival of Ottoman Turks the city started to adapt to the Islamic religion and mosques started coming up as well. Turks were pagans originally and had adopted Islam as their religion. The subsequent conflicts especially during the start of fall of Ottoman empires were signified by the defacing of the old churches and conversion to the mosques. One such historic church cum mosque is famous Hazia Sofia also known as Ayasofya. It has a huge dome and was largest religious focal point of Orthodox Church for a nearly one thousand years. Even now it is 4th largest dome structure of all the churches in the world.

When the city was conquered in 1453 the church was ordered to be converted to a mosque. The holy paintings on the wall were plastered and the structure was modified to look like a mosque. Islamic features like minarets were added to the structure. In 1935 after Republic of Turkey came into existence this structure was converted into a museum and now displays a unique amalgamation of the Christian and Islamic religion. Some of the defaced features of the church have been restored and one of the views represents the picture of Jesus surrounded by the names of Muhammad and Islam's first caliphs on adjacent pillars. Whatever was the history earlier but today it denotes the harmony and cross-cultural aspects of Turkey. Currently if one has to study experimentation on moderate Islam, Turkey could be interesting. There were all spectrums of religion scale - some very devout and burqa dad, some modern and least religious people. Like Bosporus, the legendary river that separates Asia and Europe, it provides a bridge between eastern and western cultures.

It has been the gateway to Europe and hence a center of international commerce, culture and historical empires. The city has an Asian side and one European side that are connected by Bosphorus Bridge; it is lit very beautifully at night. The city has mountainous terrain and sea cutting across to provide it with excellent scenic beauty. It was covered by a wall which was built to protect the city. As the city has long history so are multiple folklores assodated with various aspects. One such folklore was about golden triangle which was said to be named like that, since lot of gold was hidden in the sea before the invasion of the city.

The contemporary city is busy and slightly unstructured compared to other advanced European cities. In fact most part of it looked more like Asian cities. The traffic in the city was at times as chaotic as a typical Indian city. Throughout different parts in the city - one can keep wondering whether it is more of Asian or European. When we landed at the airport, looking at the racial features we guessed people were European. When one of the taxi guys picked our luggage and carried it for a distance to put it in his taxi - we said he can't be European. We conveniently settled later that may be he is a European living on the Asian side of Istanbul and hence picked up the Asian values.

Turkey is experimentation in modern Islam and that is why west looked up to it earlier for setting the stage for modern and tolerant Islam. There were parts of the city where people dressed up like any modern city of Europe; they had bars, western restaurants and night clubs, all of them. There were parts of the city where women were clad in Burqa. They had wide spectrum and surely extremes on both sides. While discussing with some of the people there I leant, there were people with ultramodern outlook and with very conservative views as well. Our tour guide, who looked one among the former category, claimed that he had learned to recognize the people and deal with them accordingly. He would know what to tell to the extremely religious Muslims and what to tell the people like us. He himself was a Muslim but jokingly he said he too wanted to visit Mecca one day on his way back from Hawaii. He thought his country was fortunate to have people like Kamal Ataturk who laid the foundation of a modern country.

While describing about the history of Turks, the Guide said - the proverb goes that three things were highly valued by them the Horse, Wealth and the Woman. One of my Indian friend in the tour pointed out that Indians proverbs also goes similar - three things have been center of all events in Indian histories and folklore - wealth, women and land (as in the saying in Hindi *"Jarh, Joru and zameen")*. The only difference was the land and the horse. Turks were the masters to domesticate the horses and made extensive use of them in the wars. The result in the history was a vast empire cutting across three different continents in Europe, Asia and Africa. The history of Turks have been full of wars, aggression and loots. The Topkavi Palace is a museum where all such memorials like diamonds, gifts and war trophies were kept from many parts of the world including India. Going through some of these sights, one can surely feel that with time civilization has become more humane; at least the gory details of war and savagery are no longer celebrated in the name of personal bravery.

Istanbul is supposed to be a gourmet's delight. They had many traditional foods in different shapes, colors and taste. Turkish delight is one such sweet that tourist buy quite often. For Indians it could be a familiar taste. For that matter many of the foods resembled Indian foods in taste. Turkish tea is one more specialty - they serve it with two kettles, one full of hot water and other with tea leaves. One such tea serving joint that we experienced was in Topkavi Palace area. It provided an excellent view on the top of a hill looking across the sea. The sight of the Bosporus Bridge was great as it was lit in different colors at night. People ended up drinking good quantity of tea, sometimes close to a liter. Turkish coffee is another specialty; it is supposed to be very strong.

The language can be a lot of challenge for Indians. I remember the struggle we had to explain the vegetarian pizza in a Domino's joint. Next day onwards we got it written on a paper in Turkish and showed it wherever needed, especially in the restaurants. There were few words common with Hindi though - most probably they had common Persian origin. So a 'chai' will also mean tea in Turkish. We realized that many a time when we could not explain things at local restaurants or shops a talk in Hindi would click, as some words would be common. Turks invaded India many times in medieval history, possibly some of their cultural and linguistic aspects became prevalent in northern part of India. It is believed by some historians that it was the central Asian invaders who coined the word 'Hindu' as they could not pronounce 'Indus'. I recall one incident when we were waiting at the gate of the Ayasofya mosque, one of the security guards asked us - which country we were from. I responded "India", but they kept asking as if it did not register. Then one of his colleagues asked "Hindustan?" - I said yes. Then they all understood. It could be an isolated case but I think Hindustan had a historical significance way back in Turkish history.

One of the aspects of visiting these old cities are the interesting stories around various things. These stories run as undocumented folklores and proverbs passed on from generations and have multiple conflicting versions.

All these stories are interesting and arouse curiosity at the pattern of lives during olden times. So there were multiple stories and versions of why Blue Mosque had six minarets, why golden triangle was called so, how St Sophia got converted to a mosque and later a museum. The character of the city is very much wrapped up in those explanations. They were different from and more interesting than the city of concrete structures and glass buildings. To me, those historical stories and sayings were interesting, much more than visiting a mall in a typical modern city. To get to know these stories as understood in the local culture makes it exciting and interesting to visit these historical places.

On socio-economic level Turkey looked similar to India. I think it looked like a developed country and a developing country at the same time in different patches. Many Turkish people migrated to nearby European countries in search of better lives. I remember one taxi driver in Amsterdam and the way he explained about the social and family values in Turkey compared to the life there. How he had not even spoken to his Dutch neighbor even once after living there for a long time, which was so different in his home country. On the economic front it was relatively on a cycle of faster growth rate and held lot of promises for the future compared to stagnant or declining growths of other European countries. Turkey with all its characteristics can surely develop as the business hub for European and Asian countries. I think language barrier could be a handicap for such things but like India, the demographic dividend is still overdue to Turkey.

Chapter 3

United States of America - one of the most common destinations of Indians

United States of America

My first trip to US was in 2005, to Atlanta. I have travelled to different cities and multiple times to US but this trip was quite eventful even before I reached there. I had a Delta airlines ticket from Mumbai via Paris and JFK to Atlanta. Delta was struggling those days with reports of chapter 11 filing and it was mostly availed for being the cheapest on the route than anything else. I was to reach Mumbai by a domestic flight at night and the Delta flight would be in the early morning. The timings of all these Europe and US bond flight from Mumbai were most inconvenient always - we had to spend an entire night at the airport and start the travel half exhausted early in the morning. The reason cited was that many of the European airports did not allow night landing of aircrafts. This was to avoid inconvenience caused to people due to noise. It was an indulgence in human convenience for selected few - if one has to compare it with the sights of taking off or landing right over the densely populated slums near Mumbai airport, at all hours of the day and night. Something which is believed to be causing so much of inconvenience to people in one country is expected to be working as acceptably fine in another country by the same set of people.

Anyway coming back to the journey - due to heavy fog, our landing at Mumbai airport was getting delayed. At some point we were told that we would not be able to land at Mumbai and the flight needed to be diverted to Goa. *"What happens to my international connection"* - I asked the flight crew? The crew member politely said that under such cases the airlines would find out the alternate routings. I already had a long journey ahead and the thought of working out alternative itself was worrying - however these were the inherent risks in air travels and not much could be done about it. Luckily, the aircraft landed after hovering over Mumbai for about one hour. Now I had another challenge - to get to the international airport and board in next one and half hour. For some of the frequent travelers, this airport transfer from domestic to international was quite a painful part of the journey. In the best possible scenario there would be a long queue of people (otherwise it was more chaotic) with their luggage, waiting to be ferried to the international terminus by a government provided unpredictable bus service. Half of the people in the queue would be impatient as they would be already late to be for their international flights. The long waiting time for the bus would not help them either. This international transfer earlier (now it is much more organized) used to add additional excitement and worry.

After waiting in the long queue for 15 minutes and free bus service not in sight, I thought of taking a taxi instead.

I spotted another worried person and both of us agreed that taking a taxi was a better decision. Mumbai taxi stand outside the airport was not a pleasant experience. I always got too conscious of not getting cheated there. These taxi drivers also knew very well the urgencies of the international travelers and how to exploit them. They asked for 500 Rs for the transfer. After haggling sometime and realizing that it was prudent to pay excess money and reach in time rather than waiting to get a better bargain, we opted for the taxi. Just few minutes after coming out of the airport road, the taxi stopped at the roadside and they started transferring our luggage to the other taxi that was waiting there. We got worried and later scared as to why they were doing so. But they did not even ask for our permission, shifted our luggage and told us to move to another taxi. It took us sometime to understand what the whole transaction was about. There were few people at the airport taxi stand who would just attract the passengers and drop them out near the airport exit from where one of their other colleague would take them to the destination. In a true business sense the airport taxi people were the 'sales and marketing folks' who just netted the passenger at high fare and later transferred them to their other colleagues in another taxi. Looked like it was a tested business model for them, but for the first timers it could be scary.

I reached the airport just in time, thanks to the taxi guy. I was the last person to check-in and board the flight, luckily I still made it in time. I thought the bad part of the journey was over when I made it to the aircraft and it took off. Soon I realized that in all this hurry I had left my ticket coupon (it used to be red paper ticket than e-tickets as today) and the boarding passes for my further legs of journeys. It was start of another trouble for me. I was confident that it should be fine since all the flight legs were in the same Delta airlines. The ticket was anyway checked at the check-in counter and fed into the system before issuing the boarding pass. Even the aircraft crew said I need not worry since it was a centralized system and based on that they could always print a duplicate boarding card. I did not have much option anyway and his argument also seemed convincing. I was pleasantly surprised when the flight landed at Paris CDG airport and even before I could disembark from the aircraft one airline official was ready with a duplicate boarding pass for me. It was the boarding pass from Paris to JFK. When I reached JFK, I was expecting a similar handover of the boarding pass for further leg, which never happened. When I requested one of the officials, she gave me a duplicate boarding pass from JFK to Atlanta.

I was relieved and happy that in spite of me losing the tickets and boarding pass, things were sorted out so easily - thanks to the centralized systems. When I was about to board the flight to Atlanta from JFK, the airlines staff asked for the paper ticket coupon (the red carbon copy that they used to collect those days before boarding). I started telling the story when the boarding staff just said politely - *"step aside sir"*. I was confident that when he would hear the entire incident, he would let me go without any trouble. Every time I requested him, he told me to wait while others were allowed to go. I waited till all the boarding was completed. In the end when I requested again, he just said I would be deboarded. Now I was in panic. The more I requested him, the more his tone got stern. I did not find him friendly at all beyond a point, not even in providing information on what should I do next. Probably, he knew only what he was doing and nothing else - not even the slightest deviation from his normal work.

I was de-boarded and left fending for myself. My luggage could not be de-boarded as it was too late for that. I saw my scheduled flight leave the airport with my luggage as I kept watching from the glass door of the terminal. All my respect and praise for systems and processes came crashing the same moment. The system was meant for routine processes only, for any small exception no one had a clue how to handle that. The only option I had was to come out of the boarding area and buy a fresh ticket. I came out of the boarding area and queued in for buying a new ticket. I was the second person in the queue - but there was no scope of showing any urgency and I waited there for one hour. I was quite amused by the response of ticketing official when I told her that she could check in the system that I was through checked-in till Atlanta. She said she could confirm from the system that I was through checked-in and collected the boarding pass till Atlanta in Mumbai - but that only proved that at that point I had the ticket with me. It did not, according to her, meant that I was still the authentic traveler unless I bought another ticket. All this proved to me that despite good systems and processes, companies even in developed countries can still render lousy services.

Somehow I reached Atlanta after buying a new ticket; my luggage had reached by earlier flight several hours earlier. Atlanta being one of the busiest airport in world, I had lost all hope of getting my luggage at the airport but was happy to find it. My hotel was close to the airport but the taxi driver asked for the minimum fixed charge of 100 dollars. In the flight, I remembered my copassenger had described how he was mugged in Atlanta one evening, so I preferred to take a safer option even if it was slightly costly.

I reached my hotel without any further incident. At the hotel I was supposed to call my colleague who had booked in another hotel and sync-up for the meetings the next day. Incidentally, the hotel phone was not working - I went and spoke to the person at the hotel reception. Since I urgently needed to speak to my colleague I requested him for the alternative arrangement. I was surprised when he said that I should call the 800 number and lodge a complaint with the telephone company. After some 24 hours of eventful journey this was the last thing I would have expected from the hotel staff. I was quite amused by nonchalant and distant approach of addressing the issue. Even if I did not expect a great service - speaking to the telephone company on an 800 number was too much to accept. I did not see much point in speaking to the hotel staff as he was least bothered. It was quite late in the night and there was only one hotel staff there. Next morning I insisted on speaking to the senior hotel staff and kind of shouted at the previous night's incident. The manager told me that the person on duty last night was a contract employee against whom there had been few complains like that earlier too. This new manager was extremely polite and had all the lessons in hospitality management. When I complained of the inconvenience caused due to phone not working, he immediately agreed to compensate that by waiving the charges of my stay in the hotel. It was too much of a compensation for me but I happily accepted it. Even without the waiving of hotel stay I was quite impressed with the way he handled my complaint and the situation there. The fee was never waived though and I too did not follow it up as it was more troublesome to get the charges reversed from the booking agent, then the hotel and the credit card company. I was better off paying the bill which anyway I could claim for my business travel.

CNN headquarter in Atlanta

Atlanta is one the largest city in US. It is famous for being headquarters for some of the big names like CNN and Coke. The downtown skyline was quite impressive. I was told however that the downtown area was not safe after evening and this was in line with other large cities in US. I don't know why the large cities necessarily have to be unsafe and infested with crimes. I recalled one of my friends narrating a story about Detroit - once famous for its auto industry and now in the news for the lack of any manufacturing activity. In the underground tube, commuters always met up with people looking like beggars asking for money. It was advisable to give them money rather than risk untoward inddent. These people were more than beggars and demanded money as if it was their right. The friend met up with one such beggar late in the night who asked for the money. He was so scared that he gave the hundred dollar note to the beggar. After sometime he realized that he was completely out of money, not even enough to buy the train ticket to reach home. Worried - he went back to the same beggar and asked for his money back explaining the whole situation. He was surprised when the beggar returned him the hundred dollar that he had given. I am sure he was different from the beggars that we are used to seeing.

Next day we had to travel to the neighboring state, couple of hundred miles away. We had some American and Indian colleague who hired two big cars for that. For a similar travel anywhere else we would have taken a public transport or in worst case, a taxi. Public transport, I learned was virtually non-existent there compared to other countries. Taxis were prohibitively expensive as well. There was some basic rail network in selected cities and bus service too but they were not considered convenient alternative to long travel. Some of the basic fundamentals like this are quite different when it comes to US. It is hard to imagine that such basic things would have skipped the exhaustive planning that they do otherwise in public infrastructure. Possibly, the Americans have got so used to cars, particularly big cars and excellent roads that any public transport doesn't make sense for most of the common people. The driving could be a pleasure on those interstate highways though - such wide roads with systematic lane based traffics - people could get addicted to driving.

These roads and bridges were the testimony of the development in United States, and truly so. This country looks so spacious, resourceful and systematic that it is a world apart from other developing countries. It is not surprising that many people get mesmerized with US - more so for many of the immigrants who came many years back.

Our car journey was quite good. The colleagues in the other car had an eventful journey though. Some distance away from Atlanta they were chased by a Police van as they apparently over-sped. The police van stopped the car and told all the passengers to come out, with their hands raised-up. They were searched thoroughly for money and drugs. The policeman later said they had information of a drug racket in Atlanta that day and hence they were extra vigilant. We have seen some of these scenes in Hollywood movies but a real life encounter could be scary. The driver of the car was penalized by reducing some driving points or something like that. These reductions in points later result into higher insurance charges for the driver and seizure of license in worst cases. Many of these systems looked fairly evolved but the police always had newer challenges to deal with, like this drug smuggling on interstate highways.

We had a meeting with a bank regarding a technology renovation project. The point to note was that the top officials in the bank were not even aware of it. The bank was about to be taken over by a private equity partner and they were assessing the takeover and its future turnaround potential by exploring outsourcing opportunities. We were invited by the private equity investor who had not revealed the intended transactions to the bank. Outsourcing project itself invoked skepticism and insecurity in US and this hostile takeover was the added twist. The challenge was to get the real picture without the bank officials suspecting anything wrong. As a precaution, we were told not to enter the bank premises in group but one-by-one. We did as told by our private equity firm and discussed with the bank's official only to understand their business and processes. They, as well as most of the other average American worker, I am sure would look at outsourcing as a great threat to their own livelihood. Something that they had been doing for years and consider their core competency and trade secret - someone from India or other developing country unravels it and transports the work to a far flung place charging a fraction of the price.

For whatever be the backlash and the politics around it, it was hard for the management of the companies to ignore this lucrative option of outsourcing at a fractional cost. If they had to make the organization more profitable, they had to avail the best possible options of getting the things done. One of the arguments earlier was that these outsourcing provided a low quality output with low productivity. That could be true when it all started, not as true later and would surely be other way round (that outsourcing results in better quality) in the future. The reason for that is fairly simple - quality and productivity are practitioners' inventions and are part of the continuous journey. Those who do the job - only they can improve the quality and productivity of what they do; it can't come from a distant theory and research. The more the work got outsourced, the incremental innovations around the quality and productivity moved to the outsourced destinations. Soon outsourcing meant cheaper cost, higher quality and better productivity. Despite the political and jingoistic fervor of protectionism (which was quite unlike America), it was hard to reverse this trend that time. India did benefit tremendously from the outsourcing boom while adding value to American economy at the same time. It did create a 150 billion USD Indian IT industry (not all of them based on outsourcing though). The recent political changes in US, rise of automation and artificial intelligence presents a newer challenge to the Indian IT companies. I think it is an opportunity for them to reinvent and move up the value chain, more as a provider of products and platform. Indian IT has now enough critical mass to lead the technology innovations in the world, however they still need to take the giant step.

Manhattan view

Years of developments and growth have put US at a vantage point compared to the rest of the world. While most of world was reeling under colonialism and poverty - Americans built a strong and prosperous nation. The nation traditionally built by the industrious hard working immigrants saw all the developments that the modern science and technology could bring in. It has also added a sense of complacency in the people of later generations who have taken it for granted. The same traditional values of hard and sincere work can be found in the common population in emerging countries like China and India today. The American people subsequently chose excessive consumerism and easy credit money to enjoy a lifestyle which was not sustainable. In an unequal and uneven world they had a good share of fortune earlier. As the globalization set in and work and fortune found its most deserving place, Americans were bound to be threatened. I always wondered how US can have corporations that are bigger than the GDP of many countries. Even the smallest of the smaller banks would have huge balance sheet there. There was a structural inefficiency brewing up everywhere in the system - a mortgage market which was nothing but the unscrupulous practices and greed of the so called best of the people in Wall Street. The people in general took it as part of American culture to perennially spend lavishly as the rest of the world produced it for them. This had to come to an abrupt end and the 2008 recession was long in waiting. I am sure this helped many nations in Europe and US to adjust to the correction in structural inefficiencies and return back to the basics to build an economy on content rather than bubbles. My view is that in the long term it is not sustainable that one set of people always produce and toil while the other set of people consume and relish. There are many findings indicating that the newer generations in the US can no longer expect to enjoy the same lifestyle as enjoyed by their forefathers some years back. Even if one does ascribe to India and China rising theory as overly optimistic - it will be hard to defend that US will see any big economic upside from here.

US will still be the largest and most significant nation but it will surely be a challenging journey for them here on. It could be more difficult than the optimism in the emerging country like India. The recent Presidential win of Trump is precisely on this backdrop of the apprehension of Americans in this new flat world.

Many times in US, I used to watch the immensely popular show where the anchor would answer the queries from the common people on whether they could afford an expensive item or a house or something else. Most of them would be already under debt with little or no savings. "Couldn't the people decide for themselves if they could afford something or not" - that they need a consultant on live TV for them to tell. Once a person who was living in US for long time explained the concept of savings - why should he save at all? If he fell ill - there would be a public ambulance to take him to a public hospital at no cost, if he lost his job - the government would offer him unemployment benefits and so on. They were covered for all eventuality it seemed. Well, the government may have money today - but the model that is based on no saving and excessive consumption, is doomed for failure. It is this same complacency that has driven many of the industries grossly uncompetitive. The fortune companies that were beacon of industrial innovation were gasping for last breath. The world noticed how the last and most celebrated financial industry in the Wall Street came crumbling down like a pack of cards during the financial crisis. I could never understand the basis of the hyper consumerism in US and wondered if it would really be sustainable in the long term.

Next time I travelled to San Francisco - the city in California known as the heart of Silicon Valley. This state is known for its affluence due to the booming information technology business. There were also stories of the dot com bust those days and how it affected the lives of many living that dream. The city by then had come out of the shadow of the recession and was right on the growth path again. Unlike many modern cities, this city does not have impressive skyline with tall glass structures. From the outwardly appearance, one can hardly say it was such a talked about center of innovation in America. The state is prone to earthquakes and other natural disasters, possibly the reason for not having tall structures.

One can feel completely handicapped if one does not have a car to move around. It is a not a city of walkers - probably very few of the US cities are. Unlike most of the big cities in Europe and Asia, public transport are nonexistent and taxis are prohibitively expensive. I understand there was a strong car lobby that ensured that such a situation continued. Most of the US cities are not tourist friendly for that matter - at least I would not prefer to rent a car and drive to new locations in an unknown city. People in India are quite used to seeing people around everywhere, it creates a sense of life and safety. Some of those wide roads had big cars plying but hardly anyone on the streets to be seen - for me it looked faceless and more devoid of life. Even for the best of the comfort and amenities it might not be as smooth for people from India to migrate and slip into the American lifestyles. For many things that they get, there could be many intangible things that would keep them thinking about what all they were missing.

Even if one wants to go around the city, it isn't as convenient. So when a friend of mine suggested that I join their family for the weekend trip to sea-beach, it was my best bet to go around the city. It was around 2-3 hours' drive to the sea front, which passed by beautiful mountains and the much acclaimed Golden Gate bridge. Like anyone travelling that place I wanted to get a photograph of the bridge. My friend said - it was one of the 'Patel Points'. He explained to me what he meant by that - the Patels, wherever they travel they make sure that they have photographs of the known landmarks with them, to show (he meant boast) to their acquaintances later. I had travelled to multiple countries by then and also at times, had taken photographs at multiple key locations - I wondered if I had covered those 'Patel Point'. I thought it was quite innocuous and natural to take photographs of such places - but I am sure some of the Indians living in US for a longer time might take it as the first time visitor getting awed by everything in US.

All along the car journey, I was awed by the excellent wide roads and bridges in the city. Then no later, I also was awed by the traffic jams on the way back to city. I thought by making wide roads they had got rid of the traffic problems - but here we were, at a bumper to bumper traffic for hours; truly, traffic was a twenty first century man made problem equally present everywhere. I was also surprised by the few beggars who would come near the car and ask for money. I was told that those homeless beggars preferred to live on the streets even when the government gave them houses. Many of them take drugs - which could be the first guess looking at them. They were beggars with a difference - but I had presumed this developed country had nothing like that.

IT revolution in the last decade has made the international travel look so commonplace for Indians, especially to the US. Earlier it was a prized travel for the selected few either for higher education or with very specialized skills. For those who travelled - it was a great thing to talk about back home. But the IT and outsourcing had broken that barrier and now thousands of ordinary Indians had travelled and been there. Thanks to the IT revolution the glorified stories of wealth and abundance in US have been seen and lived for real by many Indians. The globalization and outsourcing had also taken away the glamour value of the US lifestyle. For those singing the virtues of American lifestyle the economic recession would have come as a big jolt. I am sure many of them would have got disillusioned - as their faith in American economy and value system came under the test. Also, the same Indian friends and relatives who used to go all praise some 20 years back for life in US, they now dismiss it off as not so desirable thing. The American dream has lost some sheen in last couple of decades. Earlier, we heard stories about how desperate people would get to have the green card or get an American passport to their babies. I definitely think that some of those mindless following would reduce as people unravel America, their lifestyle, values and future that lies ahead. US will continue to remain a wealthier nation but the pie may be shrinking. The stories making headlines would not be of growing wealth but how the mightiest of the American economic symbols face stiff competition from the emerging nations. The future generation no longer looks as promising for them as the earlier ones and surely the tide is turning a different way for the immigrants hoping of great American dream. Many of them are also at a crossroads at deciding what they should adopt and what not in a foreign country, as the aspirational value of the people in everything American reduces.

Many of these Indian immigrants to US had pretty well agenda cut out for them. Once I read an anonymous article on the internet "X=X+1" - the story so well captured the state of the Indian immigrant in US. I am sure someone who went through it wrote it. The story charts out the journey of a typical Indian who goes to US to pursue his dream. A typical Indian immigrant would be an Indian graduate from a highly subsidized Indian education from IIT or other premier engineering college. He would secure an MS from one of the numerous universities in US hoping that this would open an immense door of opportunities. Given his background and earnest desire and willingness to work hard, he would get all that he dreamt. He would also flaunt it to his acquaintances in India and get the sense of achievement. Soon he would get married, and also get the coveted title of NRI. This would follow up with midlife disenchantment when he would start comparing the benefits of his current life with what he was possibly missing in his homeland. He would decide that he would surely return one day as that was what he ultimately wanted, but would keep on postponing every year that the right time would be next year. By the time his kids would grow into teens and the middle aged man would struggle to find connect with a foreign land he once so aspired. He would not be able to cut the umbilical cord from his homeland. That's why the author calls it the web of X=X+1 and many of the first generation Indian immigrants in US go through it. The story was written in late nineties but still captures the essence pretty well.

Many times I have seen old parents travelling to US, mostly unaccompanied. The occasion is also more or less predictable; it is when the Indian family in US is expecting a child. The temptation to get the child a US passport does not make it seem reasonable to them going to India where they may have better support system. The exorbitant cost of availing the complete medical facility at the same time necessitate that they call their parents or in-laws to take care of the newborn child. Once I met one such old lady at Milan airport on her way to US. Surely it was her first travel overseas and she was struggling to get the boarding instructions. Her next flight to Newark got cancelled for some reason.

I am sure she must have been told how easy it was to reach US and international air travel was no hassles at all. Here she was, not knowing what to do as the airlines official showing the least consideration gave her a ticket for next morning. She spoke to me asking for help to make an international call but I soon realized how worried she was. For the next 24 hours she stayed at the airport. As she did not have a Schengen visa, she could not be let out for overnight stay in any hotel. Talking to her, I understood how much apprehension she had for travelling alone but for the incessant canvassing by her daughter. This apprehension I saw in most of these old parents visiting their sons and daughters in US. For them, the great lifestyle in US was more of a burden than anything else - something that I could easily conclude from the ones returning from there. I realized for old parents from India, even a brief stay in US was nothing short of an ordeal, something that they wanted to escape from.

I found out that, it is not that the entire country of US is like what is projected in Hollywood movies - to major part it is conservative and family value based. Based on the image many would guess that most of US is like Las Vegas - not quite so, at least in the smaller towns. I remember once I was travelling to Madison from Milwaukee by bus. Madison is a university town and this being start of the week, the students would be travelling back to their schools. I saw most of the parents would come to see off their children and talk to them about every small thing. The family bondage in the small towns in US I think, is as good as a similar middle class family in India. What we get an impression mostly, is the life in metropolitans with broken families and dwindling family values; but that is not true for many of the smaller towns and villages.

Going through the city of Milwaukee, it appeared it must have been a thriving city at some point but now it showed signs of dilapidated mills and closing factories. That was the story of many cities and small towns in the US where the manufacturing and industrial growths have dwindled over the years. The story that gets highlighted mainly consists of the actions on the Wall Street but the small towns and villages are increasingly losing their livelihood. This was possibly one of the reasons that the palpable anger was building up amongst the middle aged Americans. They all voted to create a nationalist government that promised to get their factories back. Victory for Trump has also been an outcome of receding economic activities in small town America.

Next time, I travelled to New York - the finandal hub of the country and also the world. The Times Square, the Wall Street, the impressive Manhattan skyline are surely the testimony of the growth and prosperity. The statue of liberty is symbolic to the freedom of human spirit that America has lived through. This is a tall statue of a lady holding torch - which was presented by France in late nineteenth century. It has been one of the most noticeable symbols of US. This country that way, has been a torchbearer to the world for defining and establishing the free values whether democracy or human rights. The progressive education, research and meritocracy based general environment has attracted and lured millions of immigrants who have made it their home and furthered the developments in US. For many of industrious and hardworking people willing to change their future, America has been the best bet over the years. If one is willing to work hard, the best chance of getting rewarded is there, in the most equitable way. This has been the seed of capitalism which has worked so well over the years in many other countries. This gave rise to the free market philosophy and later, globalization. It was only last couple of years that this philosophy of merit based reward has been challenged by ire against globalization and immigration, thus diluting the principles perfected over so many years. I think it is a good reality check and an opportunity of globalization to reinvent itself.

I went to see the site of world trade center; this was post 9/11. The image of two planes crashing into the twin tower is one of the most horrifying scenes in the recent memory. In the pictures it looked small - here at the destroyed site I could imagine what a massive structure it must have been. The skyline would have been completely dwarfed by the twin towers and for the people who would have seen them come crashing, it must have been too horrifying to believe. For the attackers, they attacked the symbol of a nation - symbol of prosperity and capitalism. Whatever be the grievances this was the most inhumane act against a country. It has changed the world since then, never to be the same again. Terrorism since then has been acknowledged as the biggest threat for the future to be countered as the topmost priority. But United States' response of 'war on terror' was more of the instant reaction of attacking the suspects and the vulnerable nations to demonstrate its might.

The country is at the turning point, which is why the recent change in leadership is so remarkable. The expectation from the future is high as the recent past has been so much of disappointment for them. Only time will tell how much of it was sheer optimism and hoping against the hope. But one thing is sure that the recent events of political upheaval will change the way the Americans look at themselves and the rest of the world looks at America. Every big leadership change brings hope, Obama did as well. I recall we were in a taxi in Bucharest when Obama's oath taking ceremony was taking place. The taxi driver was so diligently listening to it over radio that he almost ignored the direction. Annoyed we asked - *"How will Obama help you even after becoming president?"* The taxi driver said - *"it was hope for everyone, including someone in far-off Romania"*.

Chapter 4

Western Europe - Growth & prosperity of the past decades

United Kingdom

I have travelled to UK multiple times, the first time I travelled may have been in 2005-06. By then, I had been to some of the countries in south-east Asia. The Heathrow airport did not present anything spectacular when compared to other airports in world. The newer airports in some of the south-east Asian countries looked more modern, compact and user friendly. The most noticeable thing about the airport was that it was very busy resulting in delayed landing and long queues for the immigration. The visitor's experience in the immigration was not the most desirable one, it left a lot of scope for improvements.

When I came out of the airport, I boarded the famous London tube- the under ground metro. I had been to such tubes/MRTs in Singapore, Malaysia and Hong Kong. Here I saw the famous London tube which was probably just a higher version of Indian railways underground. There were teenage girls looking curiously at many rats that were jumping around the track. Sometimes the rats came up to the platform, scaring the passengers.

The tracks were open unlike being covered with automatic doors in some of the countries. The train itself was quite ordinary. Most of the platforms were not necessarily convenient - with long stairs and absence of air conditioning. If one had any luggage or was unable to walk and climb the long stairs the tube could be a harrowing experience. I am sure the complete tube system must have been designed and built some 50 years ago, which would have been the best then. People could be found eating their lunch and breakfast in different hours of the day. In Singapore I was given to understand that such a thing was a great inconvenience to the fellow passengers and the offenders were liable to be fined. For the first time when I travelled by these tubes, I realized they were pretty much out of tune with their contemporary underground rail systems elsewhere in the world. London tubes needed substantive investment to be called anywhere near modern.

The iconic Westminster building

One thing that I liked about London was that it looked full of energy, a city full of walkways and squares. Whether it was the famous red bus, the tubes, the streets there would be people around, of all colors and races. If there is a cosmopolitan city, I think London should be the one. As Indian, we are used to seeing people around us all the time - crowds and queues are omnipresent. To me, it was surely a better sight than the widespread deserted looks in some of the US cities where the only mode of communication is the costly taxis. London is a city of walkers; it has a widespread city transport too which helps people move around easily. It could be a very friendly city for tourists - just take a map and move around the city - one would never hit a dead end. The names of the stations, squares and streets give the feeling of familiarity having them known through the history, movies or others. Even if you are visiting London for the first time, the city would look familiar, thanks to our schools studies and stories. There were usual sights of people singing at the tube stations while travelers giving coins to them - I was not sure whether it was a display of art or innovative begging. It is a city which can easily become home for many immigrant people. London is truly a melting pot for different races and cultures, that's the reason it is so cosmopolitan. It is a city full of life.

Every time, I have been to London, I recall the weather had been mostly disappointing. The cold weather, drizzles and not seeing the sun, can be dampening. I had studied in schools that one of the reasons of higher productivity in Europe compared to Asia, was that because of the cold weather people don't get tired easily and work longer hours. I find it difficult to believe because that cold weather can dampen the spirit and enthusiasm to come out of home and work. I think it would be difficult to wake up and go to work early in the morning when there is freezing cold, continual rain and no sunlight. It can make one lazy, contrary to the scientific statement of higher productivity. Sunlight brings the energy, warmth and so much to life.

Safety and security in public places looked quite good. I was deceived on one occasion though. I was taking a walk near a metro station. As usual there were many people around walking on those busy lanes. I find it more interesting to walk down those busy lanes rather than taking a taxi. Even though I was walking alone - it seemed perfectly fine. There was an outlet on the busy street which to me looked like a night club. There was a girl sitting on the counter inviting the prospective customers. I have been to some of these night clubs in some countries and found perfectly ok to have some drinks and spend some time. Being in the heart of the city, I did not see any security risk. After paying some 15 pounds and being convinced by asking them repeatedly that there were no other charges for the drinks, I stepped inside the place. It was a narrow staircase inside, leading to a small room. I felt alarmed and soon got scared. I realized I was in the wrong place. I wanted to go back and preferably daim back my 15 pound. I did not have options - two hefty guys almost blocked my way and asked for some 300 pounds. I panicked - I was never mugged like this earlier. They knew what to do - they asked for my wallet and took out all the money leaving some Indian currencies. It was not enough for them - they snatched my credit card, noted down the numbers and other details. By this time I was scared to the core. Looked like they were used to doing all that and it was quite procedural for them. When I murmured, that I needed the money to go back to the hotel they were kind enough to give me back some 5 pound. I came back on the street and it was a sigh of relief. I saw the police guarding the street -1 could not muster enough courage to complain or follow up with the legal complications. I cancelled my credit card in next few hours. I was sure that I was not the first case and probably it happened in some complicity of the local Police.

It could be an isolated incident and I may not be entitled to draw any generalization based on that. But shocking as it was - in the heart of the city within a crowded street - to perpetrate a 1970 kind of mugging right under the police's nose. It changed my perception of London being a safe city at least in pockets. People also suggested against the deserted subways during late hours in the night. Though the city is multi-racial and cosmopolitan, there are examples of inddents that have radal overtones. It is like any other big cities that way - it is vibrant giving an outward sense of common safety, at the same time one has to be vigilant to avoid any unpleasant inddent.

For a country which was a colonial superpower, that reigned over a large country like India for 200 years and many other countries in the world - it must be a difficult realization since then till today. It was just a couple generations back that they would have had a different perceptionof the world. The way they saw themselves, the way they thought the world would have looked at them is not the same anymore. I doubt it could be a painless transition and people will have to be magnanimous enough to embrace the new world order. Their influence has diminished in all spheres, be it political or economic. Most of them would be forced to embrace this new reality. Living with it could be more burdensome than jettisoning it. It is ironic that the British who were so entrepreneurial that they ventured into different parts of the world and ruled countries were seeking comfort in recent Brexit and opposing immigrations. From a beacon of globalization and free trade, today they are becoming increasingly protectionists. There were news articles that India may overtake the GDP of Britain to become fifth largest economy soon. For the emperors of the world - the realization of a new world order and the prognosis about challenging future, is not a great feeling. Isn't it like the aging of a famous film celebrity who slowly moves into oblivion and life gets even more difficult for him just because he was in the limelight earlier? A normal person copes with it better since he never had reached that height. A promise of a poor person becoming rich is a sign of growth and energy and an erstwhile rich society trying to hold on to slipping wealth can bring dullness and despair.

The historic London Bridge

When the European Union was created sometimes back, many people thought it to be creditable economic and political counterbalance to US influence. It did not turn out to be, mainly due to the political differences. The economic compulsion in the new world made it imperative for them to come together but the basic confrontational nature of the countries have stopped them from being truly collaborative. Europe has been most fragmented - the history is replete with the aggressions and unnecessary conflicts in Europe. Even after so many years of its formation we seldom see a cohesive view providing the leadership in world affairs, whether it was Iraq war, war against terror or any other significant issue of international concern. Their coming together looks like was more of a survival option in the fast changing world rather than world leadership. In reality, Brexit was as true since the day EU was created, just that it got formalized in 2016.

One of the common and generally inconclusive discussion point with my friends there would be - could India ever become anywhere close to a country like UK? Their infrastructure offers superior public amenities. A better regard to system and established institutions to support them are quite remarkable, compared to a country like India. One can spend time in a public park which may be as clean as private gardens. There are more people who follow the rules than those who break them. First of all, there are rules everywhere and it comes naturally to people to abide by those rules. It has been a case of planned development in most of the cases. There could be disparity but there are far more planning than chaos. In India the chaos is visible from the outset. There are some rules in the chaos too - but they may not be defined properly and there are no disincentives to break them. In India, it comes quite naturally to people to take short cuts to achieve the objective. In India, rules come into being when the chaos becomes a show stopper and becomes absolutely necessary. My view is India has lost many decades and may be few centuries in realizing that the overall system works faster if there are lesser chaos and more order. Now when it has come to terms with the world - it is changing fast. It is not taking the systematic path that a developed country took - it need not be - it can't bear with few more decades to instill those systems and rules. Growth stories at different point in time can follow different paths - so may be 17th century growth principles would be different from the 20th century ones. My assumption is, India will probably never become as systematic as a western country but that does not become a stopping point necessarily; it will be a different path to reach more or less similar goals. Indian economic growth has been mostly services lead unlike the manufacturing growth that happened during the industrial revolution in Europe.

The city of London is no doubt very beautiful. Thames River cutting across the city adds to its beauty. The sight of the river, the big boats, nearby restaurants can make for a good evening outing. Just like many countries in Europe, town planning consisted of creating squares in the cities in the earlier days. These squares which are quite unique part of the European architecture are great place to be in the evening. It is full of energy - kids skating across, families, young and old couples get together and have a good time. There would be some performers doing fire tactics or jumbling, entertaining some sections of the crowd. Many of squares would be surrounded by old architecture buildings or churches - they are signature image of Europe. These squares must have been the center of many social movements in the earlier era due to their strategic locations. I have not seen such squares in Asia or in other countries and if any, certainly they are not as lively.

Whenever I travelled to the western countries my sense of hospitality needed a redefinition; whether in the hotel or in the flight or some other places. To me - hospitality has a human face; it can't be confused by convenience that comes with the modern gadgets. An automatic vending machine can't be a comparison to someone serving a glass of water with human touch. This is where the western concept of hospitality is fundamentally different from the Asian ones. Yes, India is full of people and hence it is affordable and easy to assign such work to people rather than buying some costly machines; however for hospitality, it is much beyond this simplistic reasoning based on economic principles. It starts with the checking in the hotel - the usual greetings is replaced by a drab matter of fact business like face. Then guest has to drag his luggage to the specific room, struggle with the faulty keys at times and go through the list of instructions, like where is vending machine, how to get telephone dialing etc. Any request of help to the reception is curtly replied by repeating the instructions. It is a good idea to do the things by yourself, find your way out through all such oddities but it can't stand the test of hospitality. Self-service is also a necessity in western countries due to high cost of labor.

One incident I remember, in one of the hotel I was waiting for the check-out proceedings in London. I had to hurry but this lady at the reception was into something else and I was waiting. Every time I tried to show urgency she would ask me to wait and continue with the odd work she was doing. May be she was doing something more urgent but I was getting late for the airport as well. After some exchange of words I said, as a guest I was not happy with the way she was handling it. She suggested me to write a formal complaint and drop it in the drop box. Instead of showing any apology or addressing the displeasure, she did what she was told to do in the most business like dry manner. I did the same - not a surprise that I never received any feedback. In spite of all glorifications of 'do-it-yourself' principles, I strongly believe that hospitality is synonymous with a human face with humility rather than having some automated machines that just serves the purpose in the most mechanical way. This is one aspect where the east vs. west difference is quite perceptible. Even in some of the more developed countries in Asia, the guest experience would be more pleasurable than the London hotels.

London Taxi is a unique thing -1 have never seen a similar taxi anywhere else. It is quite spacious and comfortable for its unique antique look from outward. I was told that some of these taxi drivers are richer than the average population there. It could be true for the high fare they charge. I remember one conversation with one such taxi driver on my way to airport. He promptly came to pick me up from the hotel at 4 in the morning. Some of these conversations, I liked as they provided more information about the local culture than the books. His knowledge about India was sketchy but he was quite surprised to know that we have an electronic voting for a democracy of more than 1 billion people. The topic of discussion varied from the global warming to the London life and English premier league. I was quite surprised to know his level of understanding on all such subjects. Topics like free education, free health programs, social security and good infrastructure were the points I picked up from the conversation, which I think fundamentally separated it from a developing country like India.

Every time, while waiting at the Heathrow airport for India bound flights, one can invariably see some of the NRIs taking their family and kids for holidays in India. Many of them would be second generation Gujarati families having some business in London. The father would be allaying and answering all the never ending questions about India from their inquisitive and sometimes apprehensive kids. The questions would range from mosquito bites to people and culture. I don't think these kids brought up in English culture saw any merit in those arguments, much to anguish of the parents. I am sure the hype of such foreign residents have come down very rapidly over last few years among the Indians back home. Today, their annual holiday trips to India might not be greeted with as much enthusiasm by their relatives who would have eagerly waited for some foreign made gifts some ten years ago. Any exotic purchase from London would be a foolish decision if one can get the same thing at much lesser price in India itself. Things have rapidly changed in India in the last 10 years to the chagrin of these NRIs and their diminishing importance in Indian society. Till now they believed it was a good economic decision when they migrated to a country like Britain, but the economic prospects have changed for their relatives in India as well.

I am not sure about the statistics but predominant Asians or Indians migrants to London are blue collar, unlike US. One will find lot of Bangladeshis, Indians at the airport. They were not as many as in Middle East countries but they were quite significant. It is only off late with the rise of Indian IT and other economic sectors that white collar workers from India have started stepping in. The dilemma of migration for these newer set of people is more intense. For the blue collared workers - it is quite clear; they are there for the economic considerations and are ready to face any hardships. The softer issues of culture, identity or nationality do not worry them much. For the new generation migrants in last ten years, for whom the economic considerations are not as pressing (because they know they can get a good enough opportunity in India as well these days), these softer issues create more vacillations on identities and cultures. I remember a lengthy discussion with one of my friends who was about to apply for British citizenship. Some ten years back - he would have proudly announced this to all his acquaintances about this prized achievement. If nothing else, a British nationality itself would have been considered a passport to prosperity. But here we were - he was explaining to me why it would be difficult for him to surrender his black Indian Passport, bend to take pledge for his new adopted country. It was difficult for him for sure - more so because he is among possibly the last generation for whom it is still a dilemma - ten years ago it was not and ten years later possibly it will not be.

It is not easy to adapt to a completely different value system when the hype around the west is changing fast to a realistic realization about our own values. Take out the diminishing economic advantage of migration (due to growth in India) and the decision of Indian migration to a country like UK, can be quite debatable at least for the white collared educated professionals.

A statue of a British soldier who died in India in 1857

All of us have read so much about Europe during our school days and subsequently that it brings up a sense of familiarity with the names of the countries and prominent places in Europe. It had been the beacon of modern civilization, industrialization, democracy and liberal values in the history. The prominent incidents in the world whether it is the world wars or the scientific inventions or evolution of politics - they are all woven around the cities in Western Europe. So much have been said and talked about them that it looked like a validation of the fascinations that people in the erstwhile colonies would have. But what I was visiting, was a Europe in twentieth century. I was seeing them through the prism of history but I was not able to extend that to the contemporary world. They had great history, rich culture, industrious people and great education - but it seemed to de-accelerate there at some point in time. Things have changed quite a lot since those historical events and industrial revolutions unfolded in Europe. It would be quite unfortunate and big letdown if these countries turn out to be places of historical relevance and not the center of innovation and growth anymore.

The Netherlands

The Netherlands is one country which represents most liberal western values in many ways. It is also probably one of the best tourist destinations in Europe. The sight of the city with refreshing canals and houseboats everywhere itself is a unique experience. I learned that some parts of Netherlands are below the sea level and to prevent the water logging, the city is interconnected with numerous canals that pump the water to upper lands. It is good to see how a natural disadvantage can be converted to a great city planning to perfection. The interconnected flowing canals are the most pleasurable sight in the city for visitors. I always wondered how the water in the canal looked so fresh even when the flow was sometimes not present. Theses canals had a number of swans splashing water around or flying over each other. I am sure it would look like a great venue for the bird watchers.

The canal management is one important part of the town planning there. The canals are self-managed by the smaller communities. In the outskirts, the canals were even more beautiful. Some of the houses would open right in front of the canals where one boat would be there, like a car parked in front of the house. The outskirts are more beautiful in that sense. I think some of the quintessential sceneries on the postcards might be the real nature as seen in this part of Europe. The other very common sight in Amsterdam were the wind mills. The giant running windmills add to the beauty of the city during road travel.

A typical canal side view in Amsterdam

One other observation I had, was the number of bicycles in the city. I was amazed to see the bicydes being such a common mode of transportation in the heart of the city. I understood, most of the people had two bicycles, one at home and other at the workplace. People used bicydes extensively across the age group and economic status. It was a great idea - I wonder why many other cities do not have such a cost effective, greener mode of communication. I am sure this is also the fastest mode, given the kind of traffic in the central part of most cities. Such an extensive use of bicydes need better planning in terms of having a dedicated footpath, bicyde lane and motor vehicles pathways. The bicycles have also got a cultural acceptance there, which is a great thing. There are huge bicycle stands with locking fadlities. The tour guide told us that locking the bicyde was very important - as bicycle was a fast moving item in the thieves' market there. There were lots of bicycle thieves who quickly sold these bicydes to buy their dose of marijuana. The large number of bicycles and canals together pose a funny problem of people cycling into the canals, especially when they were drunk. The city administration had put in small barricades on the canals' side but still the incidents of cydists and sometimes motorists falling into the canal were quite common.

One of the signature images of Amsterdam are the window girls in the famous red light area. Amsterdam is known for these window girls and I was surprised to see it being such a popular tourist spot. There are red light areas in all the cities but most of them are infested with crime and fear and most importantly, there is social stigma around it. Amsterdam is phenomenally different in that sense - it is as free as it can get. The prostitution is legalized there like in some European country, but for many that sight could be remarkable in many ways; no wonder it was a popular tourist destination. On the sides of canal there were hundreds of skimpily dressed girls each inside a glass window. It seems, the word 'red light' originated from there, as in earlier days these girls used to put red bulb to distinguish it from the normal houses in the surroundings. There were walking path for the tourists who peeked into the glass windows. I think there were all kinds of tourists - young and old, married and non-married from different countries.

Most of the tourists especially non-Europeans and Asians responded to it from curiosity beyond imagination. For some of the Indians, I am sure walking on that pathway itself is a unique experience - probably because it is guilt free. It is considered a normal tourist place. There was a famous museum which consisted of all the voyeuristic and artistic collections which in a conservative society would be considered taboo. I saw the families visiting the museum and appreciating the art in the museum. This unique experience definitely suggests that there are alternate ways to look at things and this society has lived and proved that it works harmoniously as well. In a true sense of liberal values they have given different perspective to aspects that are taboo in most societies. Without getting into the good or bad or moral arguments around the same, I must say that it has evolved to an alternate working model in their society, to their advantage. I am sure the crime rates would be lesser there. Some limited amount of marijuana was also legal there in the surrounding shops. There were coffee shops where small quantity of marijuana was easily available for smoke. I am not sure, what is the reasoning behind having small amount of drugs legalized. It could be an extension to the same philosophy - lessen the control to have a better control. They might have seen good benefits of relaxing such rules in the larger context of overall well-being in society.

For the fortnight I was there, I did not see the sunshine well enough. It was very inconvenient for us to get up and go out for meetings in that cold and dark daytime. People never waited for the sunlight for their daily work. For us, who were used to seeing the sun and linking all the external work with sunlight and sunset, it was always a damp feeling. The cold did not help either. I understood why the "warm welcome" phrase had been coined - any warmth was a relief in that cold weather. When we checked into the hotel we got complimentary beer coupons for each day which we struggled to use up. Dutch are very fond of alcohol. They have very early dinner in the evening and drink from then on, even in their house.

I don't think there were too many Indians there. It was not as cosmopolitan as London. But since language is not that much of a problem as English is widely understood and spoken, it may not be as difficult for outsiders. Amsterdam is also a center of Banking and Finance. There were some Indian professionals working in the IT field. We used to visit an Indian restaurant called

'Gandhi' - that claimed that they had the most authentic Indian food in Amsterdam. The restaurant owner was an Indian who had settled there long back. He was watching Twenty20 cricket match and was so happy to see us, as he could discuss some of his views on the game. In spite of being away from India for a long time his love for the game was pretty intact and he followed it like any other Indian. It must be true for all the first generation Indian as Cricket is still a common interest to strike a conversation with. In between the match (he was listening to it on the radio) he lost the link. Since then he was calling his friend in India and getting the update every five minutes. He asked - if we were working in the field of IT? We asked how he guessed - his answer was *"who else would come so far in such cold weather these days"*. I am not sure whether it was a compliment or something else but I guessed, it was not a popular landing place for Indians whether blue collar or white collar professionals.

The general infrastructure is good, as is true with most of Europe. I remember one discussion when we were wondering how come such a small country could build such good infrastructure which did not happen in a country like India. I remember the argument of one of my colleague - *"the development in these countries started hundreds of years ago, possibly earlier. The Dutch people went all around the world, started trade, sometimes also conquered some countries, colonized them and amassed some of the wealth that they have today. They built on that advantage to further create new enterprises and businesses. Now the situation is reversing - see we are here looking for the business opportunities with them and we will as well benefit from our spirit of reaching out. A society that is entrepreneurial, is outward looking and ventures out, evolves more than those who don't."* While this was too simplistic an argument, there was a point on the merit of industrious migrant population. The countries that have progressed are not the ones who have guarded their wealth but the ones whose people have moved freely around the world creating good business opportunities. Dutch themselves were an example of that for the last century. It was due to their outward looking trading population who moved around the world, that this tiny country of few millions turned out as one of the largest economies. They have a glorious history which the Dutch must be proud of, but they may also have a sense of loss due to the diminishing stature in the new world.

There is a predominant trend of aging population in the country. Every time I travelled in the local bus, I would see mostly old people with drooping shoulders who must be sure, that the newer generation in those countries would no longer be as prosperous and proud as them. This is true for most part of the Western Europe. There is sense of listless acceptance that they are not as well equipped for the similar growth that they had earlier. They don't see a meteoric rise from here whether economically or politically. New flavor of the world is countries like China and India, for the optimism and abundant energy that their population exhibit. It is true that there is a big gap to be filled in - but the hope is that it will change for the better from now. This optimism is a better thing than the listless acceptance of the lack of it.

Glass barriers on the roadside are again a very common sight there. I understand the reason has been to protect the nearby houses from the noise pollution of running vehicles. This thought itself looked like super luxury, if we recall the number of people who live close to railway tracks in India. The country looked prosperous in many respects.

Belgium

I have been to Belgium on several short trips and stayed up to a month. Earlier, one of the weekends I travelled to Belgium from Amsterdam. Brussels has been one of the prominent cities in Western Europe. It had first shopping mall in Europe, one of the first railway lines and was foremost in industrial development of Europe. It has political significance too, as it is headquarter of NATO. There is no physical boundary between Netherland and Belgium, both being under EU; the only way the two could be differentiated as we crossed the border was the change in the color of the cows. I don't recall exactly but the tour guide mentioned that on one side of the border the cows were pure white while on other side they had partly white and partly black combination. Belgium is a very small country with around 10 million population, similar to some of the large cities in India. I was told that the unemployment in Brussels was as high as 20% which came as a big surprise to me. It had been the center of industrial revolution with industries like steel - how come it had reached that state of unemployment. It has definitely lost quite some shine from its earlier days of prominence.

Atomium - created in 1958 for world fair exhibition

Europe has been highly fragmented - into countries, cultures and languages. They have ample differences amongst themselves to have any cohesive growth. This small country is sharply divided on the linguistic lines with most of the population speaking Flemish (a variant of Dutch) and French. A very small section speaks

German as well. The language was a historical reason of conflict in Belgium and the society was split on those lines. The common saying was that if you speak French to a Flemish person, he or she might be offended. If you happen to speak Flemish or Dutch to a French-speaking person he will most certainly answer you in French with some disdain. It was safer to speak English in Belgium to avoid any such complication.

I went to the diamond city of Antwerp. One of the things that has stuck to my memory was the origin of its name in the folklore. There was a giant who used to live near the river and used to collect taxes from all the traders passing by the river. For those who could not pay the tax, he used to cut their right hand and throw in the water. This Giant had created a terror for the trading community. Then there came a boy who cut the hand of the Giant and threw it in the water. The Giant was killed. The city is named after this folklore which means "to throw the hands". This was a widely believed theory and there was a statue of the child and the Giant in the city.

Antwerp has a large Indian population that is mainly involved in the diamond business. There is a fasdnating point of view on how Indian families took over the Antwerp trading business from the orthodox Jews, who dominated this business earlier. Diamond was a Jewish fiefdom in Antwerp till 1960s, when some of the Gujarati families started migrating to Antwerp diamond district. With their hard work and willingness to excel, now the diamond business is dominated by 3rd generation immigrant Indians. Antwerp faces strong competition from diamond city in Surat which has emerged as new global center for diamond processing. Many of the Indians travelling to Brussels whom I met on flight, were diamond traders.

The city has a 19th century look - with characteristic European architecture and churches. The city - looks like has been preserved since then - it could be a delight for the tourist to have a look at the historical city. In some of these cities in Europe, I always felt like a time machine going back in time. They have been excellent in preserving the monuments and structures for their historical values. Europeans are very proud of their history and they maintain them very well, unlike monuments in India that are unkempt and suffer from lack of maintenance.

Manneken Pis which is a small statue of a little boy pissing, is one more point of attraction for the tourists in Brussels. There are multiple stories behind it. One of them goes like - a man lost his child in the city. He searched the child in every corner. He found it after two days at the place where the statue is erected today. When the father found the child he was urinating and the father made a fountain with the statue of the boy urinating. The statue is adorned in different attire every day. The size of the statue is so small that one can easily miss it.

The Grand Place square is one of the most beautiful town squares in Europe. This is central market area in Brussels. There are lines of open air restaurants serving all kind of food and local Belgian beer. They also looked like familiar sight, similar to some of the open air eating joints in India where series of restaurants would be lined up. There were people standing outside the shops soliciting the customers. Most of them offered sea food. I and my colleague were looking for a good Indian restaurant. This search kept us walking for a long time. We wanted to relieve ourselves and wanted to go to any washroom. We had to get into a restaurant without being too selective. Most of the cities in India a situation like that is easier to manage but here it was difficult. We went into one restaurant and the first thing that we asked for and went to, was the washroom. The shopkeeper was just waiting for some customer - we were the only one at that time of the day. After finishing off from the washroom we had a closer look at the food and ambience and decided not to have lunch there. At this behaviors of ours, the shopkeeper was angry like anything. We were really surprised when he demanded some money for using the washroom. Though we had no intention of leaving the restaurant after using the washroom, the shopkeeper must have thought that we tried to fool him. However, with asking for 1 euro each for using the washroom it looked like the shopkeeper was really desperate for money and he was not having good business there.

Once I asked my Belgian colleague how could Brussels manage to get headquarters of NATO given that there were far bigger countries like Germany, France etc. His answer was - the reason Brussels has been the center is precisely for that, a sweet geographical location. Since the bigger neighbors like France and Germany look at each other as competitors, Brussels came out as a natural undisputed choice. History of Europe is full of

friction and conflicts. The idea of EU was to learn from the history and come out more united politically and economically. The experiment has been a mixed success and with the rise of nationalist fervors in many countries the EU unity is in question mark again.

"I want to ask you a question, I am not sure if it is appropriate, but I am really curious to know" one of my colleague asked me in an informal gathering during my stay in Brussels.

"It is about your country, I have never been there" he added further.

"Yes - of course, please feel free to ask and I would be happy to answer" I knew the colleague quite well. I had been interacting with him for some time.

At this point we went into a corner and he asked in a hushed tone *"I watched the movie Slumdog Millionaire - Is India really like that? I was planning to visit but wanted to check with you first."*

I was not prepared for an unexpected question like this. I tried to comfort him nonetheless - *"no it is not that bad"*. Soon I realized that I was trying to tell a story contrary to the powerful projection of a movie that was winning Oscars that time. Also the mainstream media in India was shouting - we should not hide our dirt and filth, it is truth, we should not shy away. This one-sided self-inflicting love affair with negativity, unfortunately has become the politically correct narrative in Indian media over time. The media narrative do affect the image of a country especially for foreigners who have little exposure to the country themselves.

Italy

My remembrance of Italy starts with Alitalia, their national air carrier. Those were bad times for Alitalia but it was still keeping afloat somehow. It was a cheaper route to US or some destinations in Europe. Many people from India would use this airline for that reason. On one such occasion en route to Milan from Mumbai, I recall there was an announcement that all the alcoholic drinks were required to be paid by the travelers. As usual many of the travelers didn't pay heed to the announcements made in the aircraft. One of my co-passengers missed it and kept on asking for one drink after the other. He would not have imagined that a drink in the aircraft which used to be complementary always, would be payable. Towards the end of the journey he was promptly presented with a huge bill. Since then, till he de-boarded he kept on arguing with the crew. Every sip of the drink would have evaporated instantaneously for him without any hangover. I always remember this whenever I think of Alitalia. Economically, state of affair in Italy was not too far behind from its national airline - they were good at one time but slipping since then.

I have transited through Milan multiple times. Every time I was reminded how infamous that airport is for things getting flicked. These small time thieves targeted the foreigners in particular at the airport knowing that they would not raise much alarm. Foreigners not knowing local language was another advantage for these thieves. I used to be extra vigilant during the long waiting hours there during transit. Italy is known for its mafia and gangs as well but resorting to the small time theft at the airport was too much. We can always say people are more or less the same everywhere and all elements are present in all countries though in different proportions.

The mood in general in the society was not as euphoric. The general topic of conversation would invariably switch to low growth rates, closing industries, unsavory political environment and reducing job opportunities. It was still the 7th largest economy in the world and one of the key members in EU, but there was a general lack of optimism which was there even before the 2008 recession kicked in. The journey downhill can be more painful than the optimism of growth in an underdeveloped country. Some of the things they could feel positive about, were their football team and rich heritage. They had a very noisy and colorful political discourse. I read a statement by their prime minister that the women of Italy were so beautiful that they needed military escorts to avoid being attacked. I am not sure of his intention, whether he was praising the beauty of Italian women, worried with increasing crime incidents or finding work for the military in absence of any war. Possibly, he meant all the three and all of them were true while the critics called the statement sexist and offensive.

Milan looked like a dull city from tourist standpoint - the local people say it is more of business-like. It is also supposed to be the fashion capital of the world, of the fashion TV fame, but I could hardly notice anything like that. There is an old church in the middle of the city, one Ferrari shop and few shopping malls. One of the weekends I travelled to Venice and it was truly awesome. I had been to Amsterdam which is full of water canals but Venice was truly exhilarating. I had taken a train from Milan to Venice. It was a 3-4 hour journey full of the scenic beauty interspersed by lakes, ice covered mountains and green fields. Europe is very gifted that way and a long distance train is a nice experience to see the natural beauty. Some of those sceneries are very much picture perfect that we find on the postcard and always wondered if such a place ever existed on earth - probably here it was.

A walkway in Venice

The moment the train entered Venice, the experience was overwhelming. It was like moving into the sea. The great thing about this city is - it is preserved so well and gives a good glimpse of the medieval Europe, the way it would have been. It is a totally different way of life in the city. There are no motor vehicles, it is all surrounded by water and houses - mostly, old structures are erected on water. The only mode of communication there, are water-taxis that run like bus services in any other city. Most of the house doors and windows open into sea water and the water is unbelievably clean and fresh for the establishments around it. It must have been a thriving center of culture, art and religion - it still is. It also must have been a wonder in town planning and civic amenities. The city is something that will always leave an imprint on anyone who visits it - there is probably no other city like Venice in the world. The city has lot of beautiful churches and old style homes that looks like going back in time in a golden age.

Italian food is famous for delicacies and it has spread as popular food the world over. However the taste of pizza and pasta in Italy is pretty much different from what one would have eaten in India in the name of Italian food. This has been my experience with many other food specialties as well, the local version of a foreign food item is invariably so different. So even if one likes Italian food in India, he may or may not like the original Italian food in Italy.

France

Sometimes while visiting a new country or a new place, especially if the country is so much talked about in the history and so much is known about it, it becomes an exercise in validation of those assumptions or knowledge. France probably may fall into that category. Any history book of Europe is half filled with France and Germany. They have been the main constituents in Europe and continue to be so even today. They have kept pace with the modern developments and maintained their relevance in the current world. In spite of being the main architect of European Union, they have maintained their unique national identity and definitely kept pace with modern times.

Paris is quite a modern city - it is beautiful and historical too. The newly renovated airport 'Charles De Gaul' was quite impressive. The city, like any other good European city is well planned and maintained. Along with the old structures, it also has quite a few of modern glass buildings and industries denoting that Paris has kept pace with the industrial developments and still own many of the world renowned brands. While on way to the city from Airport, one can easily distinguish the patches of establishments which look more like shantytowns in various countries. These establishments had high crime rates, less education and were economically disadvantaged. I remember some of the news articles about these isolated establishments and how they have remained disintegrated with the mainstream society for years. Their denial into the general development of mainstream French population has given rise to many violent protests and clashes. They could be a close comparison to the slums the in Indian cities. When there was so much of controversy over the hyped up movie *"Slumdog Millionaire"* based on lives in

Mumbai Slums and a debate whether India is the only country having such population, I could surely relate it to such establishments in some of these developed countries as well. Though the life there may not be as poverty stricken, it can surely leave a lot to be desired. Such division in French society is not surprising. It is very difficult for an outsider to have a sense of adaptation even after staying there for a long time. That way French society in some cases are not that open to integrate and assimilate. They have strong nationalist overtone. It easily gets into 'we vs them' understanding even with a simple thing like speaking in English. For all its developments and progress, it may not be an easy place for non-French speaking expatriates. But surely, the expat population happily adapt to French way of life.

Eiffel Tower

Eiffel Tower is a monument in Paris that is truly one of the wonders of this world. I thought of using the public transport to reach the place. I thought whatever the state of the public transport be - it will surely have a good connect to that monument - which is a key tourist attraction. I was not happy with the decision later. Since everything was in French, I always had to take the help of few people who could speak English. The underground tubes looked similar to the one in London, only difference being that I was more at loss to find out where the specific station or the exit was. I had to take the bus from the last tube station to reach Eiffel tower. I was confident that I would see the structure from a distance and would not miss it. In the worst case, people at least would tell how to reach Eiffel tower and I would find my way. I missed on both counts. I saw a tall structure from a distance but never believed it could be that sought after structure. It looked to me like a normal old tower from the distance. I checked with the local shopkeepers - I was surprised no one knew about it - the problem was with my pronunciation and English language. I tried using all possible French accents for Eiffel but was not successful. Anyway somehow after walking around the structure for some time I found Eiffel tower and then I realized how mammoth it was. It is really amazing and rightly a wonder of the world for the engineering of such large man made structure. It becomes even more amazing considering that this structure was made in 18th century. It must have been a great human achievement and one can surely get overwhelmed by it.

That day when I was there at Eiffel tower, suddenly the local police started evacuating all the tourists assembled there. There was lot of confusion on what was happening there. Some people said there was a bomb scare; somewhere I overheard that there was a terrorist threat and hence the police were evacuating everyone. They barricaded the whole place, up to the main road and prevented everyone from entering the premises. It was in the evening so it resulted in lot of chaos. Till the end I never understood what the reason was but more people were talking that the place was evacuated for some film shooting which looked quite weird to me.

At night the tower was well lit and I think that was a much better sight than during the day. The area was filled up with all types of tourists and looked very lively. There were also many people selling small gift items and souvenirs. Half of them looked Indian and the other half African. Some of them were speaking in Hindi if

The Arch - Paris

they suspected that the tourist could be Indian. I have seen such people in other European countries too and always wonder how they managed to reach there and do such small errands. These people surely were uneducated lot and I am sure might not be in the best living conditions in a foreign country like France.

French society is also well known for a balanced approach towards work life. Though they were one of pioneers of industrial revolution, they equally value the importance of time that they can spend on personal and family aspects. Some of the recent regulations like maximum 35 work hours in a week and no work engagement during weekends have been due to right focus on work-life balance. This was also evident with the leisurely time spent on the weekends over long sessions of wine and food in restaurants. There is more fun to work and the French definitely exploit it well.

Germany

I have travelled to Frankfurt few times, it is primarily a business city. Since it is also one of the international air-traffic hubs so many people end up visiting Frankfurt. One occasion I remember missing my connecting flight at the Frankfurt airport due to excess fog. The arrival of the flight was delayed while all the departures happened on time - surely people would miss the flight and there were scores of them. I never understood the decision of letting so many people miss their flight and later providing all sorts of compensation in terms of accommodation, food, alternative arrangements etc. It was a nightmare for the travelers too.

I remember we stood in the queue for 6-7 hours to get the alternate ticketing. It was a complete chaos there and seeing the situation most of the airport or airline officials would not even come near us to help the travelers. I have seen such chaotic situation in many other instances at the airports. My experience has been that many of these processes are not well designed to handle any disruption or crisis. As long as the flights are on time and all processes are followed, things run smoothly - if there is slight aberration anywhere for which the things are not thought through earlier- the response gets really chaotic. All the airport and airlines official would conveniently disappear from the scene under such circumstances. They know that they will have to respond to the traveler's ire when they have no response. Also many of them would have unique problems to be addressed. I saw one elderly couple was worried that a puppy was with them and they didn't know what happened to it due to these cancellations. The puppy needed food and someone had to attend to it. Another person wanted to attend his mother's funeral and had to somehow be in India within next few hours. Each of these travelers who looked so innocuous and happy otherwise had a different case in point that comes to light only under such circumstances. I pity those officials who were trying to control the crowd. I am sure that they would not have any answer to many of these problems. This is one of the disadvantages of being too accustomed to systems and processes. That way Indians are more accustomed to such chaos and I think somehow they end up managing it little better.

A heritage monument in Frankfurt

I was told that there was nothing great to see in the city in Frankfurt. But still it made sense to go around the city since I had the opportunity. I took a train to the city's central railway station. It was quite evident that we were a bit out of place as foreigner almost everywhere. The public reaction was surely not as receptive and our unfamiliarity with the local language always made matter worse. Even after having a map of the city and train routes, we were always struggling to find where we were and how we could reach some destination.

I guess it may not be easy for the immigrant Indians and Asians to get around the city and do business as usual. I always thought that in spite of being prominent

European nation, Germany was a less cosmopolitan society. I did not have a longer stay in Frankfurt or any other German city, but my first impression was that it might not be the best place for Indians to migrate. Thanks to their industrious population and a focus on engineering, Germany has been as prominent country politically and economically. They are as relevant today has they have been in our history books.

Germans have been very successful at the marvelous engineering and continued innovation in various areas. Their focus to detailed planning has been exemplary. In one of the organization that I used to work, my team mates could easily tell if the presentation was prepared by a German. It would be so detailed that sometimes it would be overwhelming. I was told they follow a bottom-up approach of planning more often. Similarly it is a tough task to convince a German manager if one does not have a complete plan. A plan is not to be executed unless everything is detailed out. So if you are a top-down problem solver and have a German boss, the work situation can be tricky.

Denmark

Denmark is one of the most prosperous nations in northern Europe. This country of 5.5 million people is supposed to have the most equitable income in its population and one of the "happiest place in the world" - as per some survey based on the standard of health, education and welfare. Some surveys have also put this country as one of the most peaceful and least corrupt countries in the world. During my two weeks of stay in Copenhagen all these statistics did seem to be true. The city in the residential area is very peaceful, sometimes to the extent of looking deserted. The city is beautiful and systematic by all accounts, presence of sea and canals adding more beauty to it. The houses are structured and systematic - of similar heights, color and formation, typical of European cities. No wonder Copenhagen is found to be one of the most common places for international conferences.

One noticeable feature of the transport in Copenhagen was the use of bicycles. Of course the public transport consisting of the trains and buses were extensive and good, but the use of bicydes throughout the city was quite rampant. All the roads would have a cycling path and the city was more accessible by bicydes. The central railway station was modified to construct two floors of parking for bicydes. I was surprised to see the parking stand for bicydes inside the trains. It took me some time to realize how easily the bicycles can be fitted in those stands. Even most of the cars were fitted with the hook at the back in which a bicycle could be fitted in and carried easily to far-off places. A sizeable population uses the bicycles to come to office as well. In one of the tours, we were told that Danes are very environment conscious and the use of bicycles was just one indication on the same.

On one end there were people who used bicycles to commute to work, on the other hand there were few people (I met one) who every day commuted for work via flight. Coming to office daily by flight was quite a unique revelation for me. Being a small country that Denmark is, I never could believe this. Denmark is geographically divided into the landmasses in the linear structure so some people stay far off and commute to office daily by air.

Statue of Little Mermaid - arguably the most photographed statue

One of the most famous things in Copenhagen is legendry sculpture of "the little mermaid". Arguably it is the most photographed lady on earth. The story goes like the little mermaid falls in love with a prince. She wants to give up her life as a mermaid and live a life like human for the prince to accept her. She goes to a witch and the witch gives her a potion. After drinking the potion the mermaid loses her tongue and becomes mute. She gets the legs though it pains and bleeds a lot when she walks on the land. The sad end of the story is that the prince does not love her even then and she keeps on waiting. There have been multiple versions of the stories with some disputes but all agree to the sad end. It is a small dark statue on the sea shore on a big stone. There was a small gathering of the tourists and they all were taking photographs with the statue. To - me it looked similar to the 'Manneken Pis' statue in Brussels. If one takes away the story behind it, there was nothing spectacular about the sculpture. It was as ordinary as it could be. One of the Danish friends told us that the little mermaid would be sent to China that year for some world exhibition. More than anything, he was worried if Denmark will get the same statue back or too many of them given the China's reputation for copy and mass production.

We took a tour of the city. In the open roof bus - it was well organized. This is one good thing about many cities of Europe that they are quite tourist friendly. They have preserved the monuments, landmarks and historical structures and mostly have a convenient package tour around them. This tour also was well organized with details about the history, war monuments, social life and Christianity. We realized that the area that they were going around was small and looked like they were small concentric circles that different tours operate. Anyway it is not a big city, so most of the landmarks were close by.

At one point the tour guide showed us the yellow army style barracks with the windows that were infamously used by the wives of the army men to wave and call in while their husbands were away fighting the wars. It also showed the old locality of Christiana which was a different belligerent establishment and where the laws of the land were not followed. Another famous landmark is Tivoli Garden which is an entertainment park. It was lit very beautifully in the night. It had beautiful garden consisting of the tulip flowers. It was freezing cold when we went there at night so I am not sure if the day-visit would have been better.

In the evening while going through some of the busiest streets I was surprised to find the set of young people smoking grass in public. In fact it was quite open, where many young teenagers were sitting by the side on the road and making cigarettes by taking out the tobacco and putting in the grass fillings to smoke. It looked like a party spot - I am not sure if that was a legalized drug spot but it was surprising that it could be done so publically.

Once inside the residential area, the place was quiet and serene. There was absolutely no noise or any other sound of kids playing or vehicle noise during the day or evening. No wonder the people in Europe take exception to flights at night. The residential area could be so quiet that at times it was like a silence of uninhabited areas of jungle. It was hard to find it lively that way. May be these things contribute significantly to the best standard of living in Copenhagen, but it was surely devoid of the dynamism that we as Indians are used to in a human surroundings.

Any discussion on the family and social aspect could be tricky for Indians. I later understood that the Danes do not appreciate it as much too. I was chatting with one of the Danes - he said he has 4 kids ranging from 28 years to 11 years. Further discussion got into how many of them his wife had from previous marriage and how many in the current marriage. There was no difference between the live-ins and marriage I was told, except some small aspect of legal provisioning. I asked what age is that typically kids leave the parents' homes. *"As early as possible"* - was the candid reply. The kids are encouraged to stand of their own as early as possible. Almost all the older parents stayed at the state provided old-age-homes or their own homes if they had earned and saved enough but in no case with their grown up sons or daughter. It looked quite simplistic social setup that way and that's what years of prosperity would eventuality grow into. So it is no wonder that even in India some of these nuclear families are getting more and more prominent as the prosperity come in. The people in European countries are ahead on this path probably. Much of it has got to do with the economic independence than the cultural aspects. Only thing is the phase of the transition brings in lot of confusion and disputes.

Looking for map - A typical street in Copenhagen

Cost of living is one of the highest in Denmark even among the European cities. For all the peace and prosperity there was a premium to pay. It had its own Danish language. Denmark had own currency that they had not changed though they were one of the main architects of EU. The Danish people voted against the use of nuclear power in a referendum. They are peace-loving people mainly. Incidentally they became famous earlier because of the 'Danish Cartoons' which was so unlike their peaceful nature. It was not something that an average Danish would have been happy about - getting known to the world for provocative reasons.

Chapter 5

Eastern Europe - Similar but fragmented

Georgia

When I first enquired about my air ticket to Georgia, I realized I was given a ticket to Georgia in US. I was supposed to visit Georgia, the breakaway state of Russia which was more in news because of the so called conflict with Russia rather than anything else. I was visiting their capital Tbilisi for 2-3 weeks. I had done the hotel booking on the internet and had also asked for the airport pick up, as the landing time was around 2 am in the morning. I had spoken to the hotel people to ensure that they be there for the same. I was transiting via London.

When I landed in Tbilisi it was freezing with subzero temperature and the chilling wind. It was an extremely small airport with very few ground staff at that odd hour. I was the only Asian in the small ATR aircraft from London. While clearing my immigration, the official told me to step aside to deal with a complicated visa validation process. I think for British citizen they did not require visa so they were allowed to clear immigration easily. I waited till the end and then I realized I was almost alone at the airport. The visa imprints on my passport were in Georgian and even the immigration officer was not talking English. I was told that he would be having a copy of my visa endorsed by their commerce ministry. I had to wait for some more time on that deserted airport talking to the visa official in sign language before he located the approval letter sent to him. It was great relief to me to get the things sorted out. I was scared to think if the hotel pickup somehow missed. The airport was deserted - not many flights land there at that odd hour. When I went to collect the luggage there was only one suitcase left and luckily it was mine. Fortunately, the airport pickup person was waiting for me inspite of all the delays and I finally reached the hotel safely.

A street in Tbilisi

The city had all signs of an erstwhile communist regime - the thick stone constructed buildings, the general architecture, roads and bikes. It will be very difficult to differentiate it from a small city in Russia. I learned Stalin was born in Georgia. The country is trying hard to come out of its communist past. I was surprised to see the kind of animosity that they had towards the Russians. For most of the Georgians, Russia was an aggressor and they had many historical instances to support that belief. According to Georgians, Russia threatened their very existence. When recently I read the news of the war between the two - I remembered that their animosity ran very deep. The Georgians consider the Americans as their friends. It was only based on the principal of common adversary rather than any benevolence of America for the Georgians.

The hotel that I was staying, was a small one - it did not look like having too many people as tourists. There was a small bar in the basement of the hotel where we (along with a colleague of mine) would go and have drinks. I guess, we were the only guests in the bar for those two weeks that we stayed there. The bar too was not used to having too many people as guests or maybe it was due to the off-season for tourists. Once two of us were in the bar, as usual discussing about the events of the day. The hotel staffs were having parties - few of them around 5-6 people. It was some celebration for the completion of the number of years for the hotel. By then we had become friendly with the bartender as we were the only customer for last few days and she would exactly know what all we would order for.

My friend enquired - whether they would invite us for their party. "Why not" - they said and we joined their team as we had nothing better to spend time. It was a long session of drinks. There were 2 ladies and 3 men in the gathering. Only the ladies spoke English and our conversation was restricted to them. One of the lady I was surprised to hear, knew some old Hindi Songs - of Raj Kapoor's era. She sang those old Hindi songs verbatim, it was great to hear. I had read that Indian cinema was popular in Russia but it was quite surprising to see a

Georgian girl singing when she could hardly speak English, leave aside any bit of Hindi. She had a son and was divorced - from what she narrated it did not seem that the social condition of women was that great.

They had a unique way of drinking 'Tequila'. In a party everyone starts the drink in a small glass and finishes at one go. This they do in a synchronized way with all in the gathering multiple times during the session. Refusal to the drink by anyone is not considered good social etiquette. After 2-3 rounds of the strong drink this social acceptability became difficult to carry further for me. They said they take great pride in hospitality of the guest and that's why they invited us to their gathering. They appeared culturally closer to India. Tbilisi was also a center of education and some Indian students used to travel there for studies. Of course, this was during earlier days of USSR when India was politically closer to Russia than the rest of the world.

Street view on a sunny day in Tbilisi

We had multiple meetings with the officials of a bank there. I remember vividly the room that we had the meeting. It was a wide stone building of earlier era. The lift taking to the meeting room, was something that we don't see now-a-days. It had heavy iron grill as the lift door - which could only be opened and shut by a well-built fellow Georgian. The meeting room would be cold like anything and we had two small room heaters (one of which I would try to keep strategically near me). This pretty much summarized the state of other infrastructure that they had too. From what it looked - it must have had been a good infrastructure 50 years back. Since then the time has frozen - things have not changed too much for their betterment.

We wanted to tour the city. It was not a frequently visited tourist destination. The hotel staff told that people usually take the river cruise which shows various landmarks in the city. It was off season for such river cruise, the hotel staff suggested but we still wanted to go ahead for the lack of any other better alternatives. I had been to Nile Cruise earlier and hoped it would be a similar experience. The cruise was fixed for one of the evenings. My colleague and I reached there in time.

I could not believe when we boarded the huge multilevel boat and it was just two of us. I never expected a large gathering but I surely expected few more people on the cruise. The lights were switched on wherever we went, the guide asked us if we would want to visit the bar then he would set it up. It was quite an anticlimax for what I was expecting. He took out the huge cruise boat for just two of us? I am not sure if it would have covered the cost of the fuel for his boat. The boat owner (cum guide) was quite enthusiastic though in showing all the landmark of the cities as he undertook the tour. In the 1.5 hour cruise he took us through the brief history of the country, the neighbor disputes, Russian aggression and US friendship. He also asked a lot of things about India. I remember some of our answers surprised him, like how can one country have so many religions, so many languages and still be one country. So, much of diversities which come naturally to us - was not conceivable for him. After this incident I was wary of the 'off-season' caution for trying out something like cruise in any country.

One of the days before the start of a presentation I projected a photograph of Tbilisi streets partly covered in sun. One of the lady, part of the presentation quickly commented

"Isn't my Tbilisi beautiful?"

I replied - *"Yes it is beautiful"*.

This sentence resonates in my mind whenever I think of Tbilisi - "Isn't our Tbilisi beautiful" and that is what I would remember it as and am sure so would others who would have visited it.

Romania

To get business visa for east European countries was never easy - Romania was no exception. One mandatory rule was the physical appearance for the consular interview in Delhi. I don't know if I was one of the rare person looking for business visa from India to Romania, going by the range of questions during the interview.

Business district in Bucharest

I have visited Romania multiple times. It is a relatively large European country catching up fast in terms of development. It has been under communism for more than 40 years and only recently moved into a democracy with market economy. Due to higher growth in Bucharest, many of Europeans were buying houses and thus driving the realty prices high. Lot of such buying must be speculative only, because I don't think Bucharest provides any cosmopolitan experience for the expats to make it home. Not only the Indians and Asians even the European from other countries would find it difficult to live in Bucharest. The difficult visa and work rules in some of these countries make things difficult for Indians even more. With such policies I doubt it can ever get integrated and be a vibrant progressive economy. All the big cities in the world are more open and inclusive.

One of the most famous thing in Romaniais its parliament building, which was built by the communist dictator Nicolae Ceasuescu. He ruled Romania under communist regime from 1965 to 1989. This is a gigantic building with an area of 65,000 square meters. It is arguably the second largest building in the world after Pentagon. The story about this palace pretty much tells the recent history of Romania in the context of communism. The communist dictator wanted to create a massive structure as a pride for the country and hence ordered all the materials to be created from Romania only. To build this structure thousands of houses, churches, schools and hospitals were demolished in the heart of the city. He employed thousands of workers and hundreds of architects who worked for four years to erect this huge structure with seven huge floors and many underground floors. While the premier splurged money on building this structure, the common Romanian population suffered for the lack of the basic amenities. He did not live to see his dream of seeing this building complete though, he was captured and executed on the Christmas day in 1989. It is not a coincidence that how all these dictators once considered so powerful and revered, meet such tragic end. This palace, for most of the Romanians, summarizes their recent past and a mixed feeling of pride and apprehension.

There were not too many Indians to be seen there. I recall one incident when we were in our rented apartment, we heard a knock at the door. When we opened the door, we saw a person with a lady. He overheard us talking in Hindi and knowing that we were Indian could not resist meeting us. He was half drunk but I found some of his conversation very interesting. He was very excited to talk to someone in Hindi in a country like Romania. He was apparently born in Kenya, brought up in London and now an American citizen living in New York. Hardly anything about him can be called Indian, other than having Patel as his last name and understanding Hindi and Gujarati that he picked up as kids. But it was he, who went at length to explain how he has an Indian blood if nothing else - I wonder if it is only Indian origin people who feel so much of pride with their Indian-ness.

He was earlier with American Air Force and part of the Iraqi troop for which he did not have any kind words. He said he kicked his American air force job as he did not like and agree with what he was supposed to do. In his own words - he was made to destroy the lives of poor Iraqis and he was better off in his new job with the World Bank. He offered to have beer with us and go to the night clubs in Bucharest. It is not an easy city to go around at night, especially if one does not know the local language. I recall few times our colleagues being accosted by the local police and searched for valid travel documents. So, in general we avoided travelling outside unless necessary. He must have felt let down when we politely declined his offer of pub hopping. That did not deter him anyway, he was enjoying life in Bucharest on his own terms.

Eating out in restaurants for us was not a preferred option. There were not too many Indian restaurants also. Some of these situation, my MTR packets came very handy. For short duration trips of 2-3 weeks, these prepacked Indian food were very helpful. All one needs to do is to heat it up in boiling water for some time. It was quite convenient, especially when I reached hotel at odd hours and the kitchen services would be shut by that time. The only challenge sometimes with these packets were while dearing immigration into the country to explain the contents of the food. Some places I got weird look from the immigration officials as why someone would ever carry pre-cooked food during international travel. For frequent travelers cooking is a must have skill, especially if one is particular about specific types of food. I recall when we travelled in groups for longer duration, the team members with cooking skills were most sought after.

Eastern European countries have some similarities within them and also a marked difference with their western counterparts. They have been the poor cousins of Western Europe in some sense. They had all the common malaise of Europe like fragmented smaller countries with conflicts amongst themselves while lacking the development prevalent in the western part. They had lagged in the development that happened in countries like France and Germany and were still waiting to catch-up in spite of being in EU. Some of them had been caught with communism and are now slowly trying to emerge out of it, but it would be a long catching up for them.

Croatia

I remember visiting Croatia some time in 2005. It is a small but very beautiful country. It could be a must see place for people who enjoy the nature's beauty. Zagreb, its capital is a small city by any standard. It is surprising that in spite of being good tourist destination it is hardly known that well. The smaller airport of Zagreb was not used to seeing many different faces, certainly not many Indians. When we went for the immigration clearance, the official there made us to wait in different queue while other Europeans were cleared without any hassles. They were definitely not used to seeing many Indians, rather my view has been that they find it so unusual that they get suspicious most of the times. It was rather unusual for them to believe that there could be some legitimate reason for us to be there and hence most of the time we were subject to greater scrutiny. Not many Indians would go to Zagreb for holidays, least of them for business.

That was the next morning of the London Underground bombings, so the airport authorities were extra vigilant. One of my colleagues and I were asked to step aside and wait while the others were cleared by immigration. We waited and waited for next one hour and every time we went to ask why we were made to wait - we got no reply and asked to wait some more time. The language also made the things difficult for us to understand what was happening there. After one and half hour of waiting, two of us were called inside a room. We saw our local business partner was called at the airport. The business partner was furious as he had to come back from a holiday resort to attend to us. He told us later that there was a local rule that for business visits, the local partner needed to be there to receive the visitor in absence of which the immigration officials were planning to deport us. What a weird rule - I could never get an official account of the incident. My immigration experiences in most of such east European countries have been less than pleasant but this was quite scary.

A beautiful heritage castle in Zagreb

Croatia is small country of less than 5 million population. Life seemed slow moving or dull from outside. It had come out of a long war and seeing peace in recent times.

It is also surrounded by nations like Serbia, Bosnia Herzegovina and Slovenia that have been fighting wars till recently, only to give peace and development some chance thereafter. The reasons of some of these conflicts were so deep routed and complex that any analysis could be risky of being superficial. There are not too many things in Zagreb to see but some of the nearby places are worth visiting.

One such place is Plitvice lakes national park. It was couple of hours' journey by bus from Zagreb city. The bus ride in countryside Europe is always enjoyable and this one was no exception. The villages on the way looked so beautiful - away from the relative hustle and bustle of the city and still having all basic amenities (unlike Indian villages where basic amenities like water, road and electricity are absent), they can be ideal place for peaceful living. Plitvice lake that I visited consists of multiple lakes surrounded by mountain and a good amount of plantation. It covers a large trekking area covering the lakes, mountains and the trees. The lakes are interspersed with numerous waterfalls that make it a great natural sight. The color of the lakes change based on the sunlight, amount of minerals and vegetation around it. Some of these sights are picture perfect in true sense. One thing, I was impressed was the cleanliness of the area. Though it was frequented by thousands of people every day and had a long trekking path, it was immaculately clean; not even the chocolate wrappers were thrown around. This is something that tourist places in India need to improve upon, especially at the natural scenic places.

Chapter 6

Australia & New Zealand - Gifted with abundance & natural beauty

Australia

I have always found that the first conversation with the taxi driver in a new country while travelling from the airport to the hotel, is more informative than the loads of pamphlets to promote tourism. Most of them are more than willing to talk and share their views about the country and its people and they are quite real I think. So when I reached Sydney after a long flight from India, I was happy to chit-chat with the taxi driver on my way to Hotel. The taxi driver was a Bangladeshi and was keen to talk about various aspects of life in Australia. Of course, he was looking at it from an immigrant's perspective. Most of the taxi drivers in Sydney are from South Asian countries. I also understood that many of the students who come to study in Australia take up part time jobs like taxi driving. I could later relate it to some of the crimes that were reported against the Indian taxi drivers, few of them being students.

It was a recently concluded cricket tour by India - where Indian cricket team had beaten Australians in their own country. The topic found good resonance in interest for both of us. *"This time Australians had the taste of their own medicine"* -1 think he was talking about the unnecessary aggression on field. We went on discussing about the same. Those were the heydays of Australian cricket that were marked by the aggression of an invincible team. I don't know why many people wanted to see the end of domination of international cricket by the Australians. Not only was the domination getting predicable and boring but also uncomfortable for cricket followers. So, beating Australian team in Australia was a rare event to feel happy about and many of us echoed the same view.

Then the discussion turned to work. He told me that the tax system in Australia was enacted in a way that it discouraged excessive working, whether for the taxi drivers or others. All working hour beyond the stipulated hours in the week were taxed very heavily, hence some immigrants like this taxi driver, was forced to the lower working hours. I remembered the 35 hour week rule in France and much controversy about changing it in current scenario. Such rules could be acceptable if the particular society has reached a saturation point in well-being and believe that they continue to be there in future. I am sure there would be valid reasons behind such rules, but for immigrants who were willing to work extra hours, this was more of a nuisance.

While we were discussing about various things he said that we were approaching a viewing point that people love to see when they first time come to Sydney. It was a signature image of Sydney and Australia. The well-lit Sydney harbor bridge at night really presents a spectacular view and one of the most memorable sights. The adjacent Opera house adds to the beauty of the bridge. The view one can easily link up with the New Year celebration each year with the fireworks revealing spectacular view of different effects in sky above the bridge. We crossed the bridge and approached the hotel - the roads were really deserted by late evening; it appeared as if the city sleeps quite early. I thought Sydney being a large city would have a more active night life. I was told most of the city is safe even though deserted at that hour.

When I reached the hotel, it was one of the most unique experiences of checking in. I have been into many hotels in different countries but this one was quite unique. I had done the booking through internet, therefore had not much idea about the hotel. There was no one at the entrance and the door was locked. There was an instruction though that I should press one button to speak into a speaker phone. I did that, and the remote voice confirmed that I had a booking and opened the door electronically. Inside too there was no one. I came back and talked into the speaker phone again - I was told where my keys were and where was the location of the room. I missed direction to my room and came back to talk into the speaker phone. This was the third time I was speaking to him and his irritation was visible. He explained to me the direction again followed with a succinct hint - *"if you don't find the room this time or the doors don't open don't come and ask me again"*. After much struggle I was able to find the room and unlock it (it was in an adjacent building). I was quite surprised with the completely automated and faceless check-in. It was around 10 pm at night and I thought that was not so late to risk such inconvenience to the visitors.

A view from Darling Harbor - Sydney

In my school days Australia was a tricky question whether it is a country or continent. It is another name of abundance when it comes to land and nature. With 20 million population and a landmass as big and rich as it has, I wonder why it is not one of the best places to migrate for people who yearn to see sun and sand. For Europeans it is definitely one of the best places to migrate to. The morning view of Sydney Harbor Bridge is so refreshing - the boats ferry in crystal clear water in the bright sunlight. It could be probably one of the least polluted cities in the world - clean and bright. The skyline is impressive and not as cluttered as some of the other large cities in the world. The nature and wildlife is probably preserved in one of the best possible way. The weather is nice most part of the year - I am sure Sydney would be one of the most preferred destinations for quality of life. Only disadvantage could be it is in the middle of nowhere. Australia geographically being located where it is; is a long distance away from other countries.

On my way to Australia, my co-passenger who was British and had been to Australia multiple times said - Australia is the best place to migrate if you are British. I don't know if her statement summarizes and is representative of general life in Australia. She also said that many of the whites migrated to Australia from South Africa when the apartheid ended there. Australia has been in news for various incidents having racial overtones. Its own record with the treatment of what they call lost generations has been subject of various debates.

Most of my interactions with fellow Australians have been quite positive. A typical Australian is quite jovial and friendly. One incident I remember when we were coming back after completing a business meeting. It was a very crucial meeting and we continued with the discussion points unraveling each point and what the client meant or hinted. It was quite intense discussion, 3-4 of us continued discussing it even in the lift on way back. One Australian who did not know anyone of us and had no clue what we were discussing - suddenly pointed to one us and said "I fully agree with you but

I have a point". Before we could react, he left but not before we broke into laughter. I think his message was very clear - *"guys take it easy, nothing in life is as important and crucial, surely not the work".* I think this attitude is noticeable in many other Australians - they don't stretch too much for work, not even under exceptional circumstances. Weekends for them have got nothing to do with work. They would be more interested to pursue their hobbies like bike racing and Yachting or other outdoor activities.

Legendarij Sydney Harbor Bridge

Ferry ride in the clear water is very good experience near Darling Harbor. The multitude of the yachts and racing boats in the surrounding water present a nice view. I went to Bondi beach, the much acclaimed beach in Australia. It was very clean in spite of being so crowded but I could not differentiate it otherwise from other beaches. The other good beach is Manly beach - it has a very good walking path covering the beach. With all such attractions Australia is a very good tourist destination. Most of its attractions are natural, not to speak of the wide spread- out country sides inhabited by kangaroos.

A waterfall in Blue Mountains

One of the weekends I went to visit Blue Mountains. It is couple of hours train ride from Sydney. It is one of the most scenic places and very well organized for nature tourism. I walked around the place. I had read news article about how many people get lost in the dense forest of the mountains and sometimes remain untraceable for days and months. The forest was also prone to frequent fires. It had a very beautiful waterfall. The cable car ride was a nice experience as well.

Sydney has a population of less than 4 million - fairly small compared to the other large cities of the world. It is widespread, I thought it had enough area for everyone to live. It still has the problem of growing housing cost and is one of the costliest cities in the world. It is also one of the most livable cities as per many international surveys.

New Zealand

I have travelled to New Zealand three times - twice to Wellington and one time to Auckland. I am sure, I must be few of the business travelers to New Zealand that is outnumbered by the holiday tourists. It is a perfect destination for that - quiet and serene at one end of the world. The long sea coast, hill station like cities, vast green land, a laid back population; it has probably all that a holiday seeker can look forward to. I first reached Auckland which is the international airport. From Auckland there are continuous flights to Wellington but they quite depend on the weather of the city. Wellington is a city on the hill and people can see all possible weather changes in a single day.

When I reached Wellington I was quite exhausted due to the long air travel and jet lag. This time I came across a Pakistani taxi driver. He seemed very interested in talking to someone from India. As I discussed with him further, I learnt he was from Punjab in Pakistan and came to New Zealand some ten years ago as a student. His father was a high ranking government official in Pakistan and he came here long time back in search of good life. In his own words "had he been in his own country - he would be running a respectable business and most possibly be much well off". This is the irony of immigration - many a time a distant life which looks so promising gets quite illusive later. His achievement could not be exaggerated - after doing his masters from a local university in New Zealand - here he was, driving taxi. For few dollars that he was earning, he thought he was paying a big price being away from his family and friends. *A million dollar or invaluable"* - he said he thought was the price of having dinner together with his extended family including parents, siblings, uncles and aunties. Surely the price tag was high since he had been away for so long but he was talking about the pangs of being away from his near and dear ones. Why does not he go back then -1 asked him? He would go back he said - next year may be, and for good. I am not sure whether he was in the web of X=X+1

"Will you not miss this country and city where you have stayed so long?" I asked.

"Not a single day my friend - this city is nothing but a big village", he said. *"May be I will miss my university days but nothing beyond that"*.

I said - *"one good thing is people are very systematic, they follow rules, traffic - it is good thing to have"*.

He had different view on the same - *"it is not respect of rule or law that people care for there. It is fear of rule. It is the strict enforcement of mechanical rules - just relax the rules for few days and you can see how wild these people can get"*. He contrasted that with his view of his country. There were no strict rules there, even far poorer enforcements, people still behaved and were courteous to each other. There is the respect of societal values. One is very conscious of his social stature and that governs his behavior. He would fear his God to do right things and hold the respect of his parents and relatives. This was sometime in 2006-7 when Pakistan was not as worse and chaotic as it is today. His sense of pride and affection were still fondly linked with his home country and culture. He was surprisingly disengaged with a country and culture where he had been for a long time. Looked like he was a devout Muslim - I am sure he could never flaunt his religion publicly there. For all such migrants - there must have been an economic reason earlier which could compensate for the stress due to different value systems in a new country. The economic reasons sometimes do not work out well, as in this case; at times one can land up on the wrong side of prosperity and it could be frustrating.

New Zealand Parliament - Wellington

Till the time I was in Wellington the 'Big Village' kept ringing in my ears. It is quake affected city and I learned, every year there were hundreds of earthquakes there. That is probably the reasons that there were not too many skyscrapers. The skyline was more beautiful though, with the houses on the hills and cold cloudy weather mostly. It must be a wrong city for business travelers - it is for the holidays surely. New Zealand provides holiday of a different kind - leisure, not like crowded tourist cities. There were not too many tourist spots or historical places to see. I think most of New Zealand is like that. It is favorite for the western holiday seekers who can slip into the countryside in the natural surroundings and take some time off from the crowded cities.

New Zealand often gets referred to as an addendum to Australia which Kiwis don't appreciate. There are many jokes that the people of either country talk about, only the butt of the joke changes based on who is telling. I found Kiwis were quite friendly, cheerful and respectful to the foreigners. During the spate of attacks on Indian students in Australia, New Zealand came out with a tagline to attract these students - *"we are different from Australia in the nicest possible way"*. I think that was true to a great extent. They are more humble in general and do not exhibit as much of aggression.

I very well remember the gesture of our local business partner inviting us for a cake cutting ceremony and small celebration on India's Independence Day. No other business partner in any other country I remember extending such invitations. One of the common topics of discussion for us was cricket surely. For the size of their small country, they are a good sporting nation for many other sports as well

Sky swing Rotomvn - New Zealand

Most of the people go to New Zealand for holidays and that is what it is best suited for. During our last trip we planned to go around the city along the countryside, which was supposed to be one of the most beautiful. So, we rented a car (Indian driving license was accepted there) for two days long drive to nearby cities. The countryside is truly picturesque - green hilly mountainous farms spotted by grazing sheeps in the nice cool weather.

There were snow covered mountain peaks on the way. There were thermal valleys, where steams would keep coming out. There were some volcanic mountain regions as well. The drive was perfect pleasure amidst the natural surroundings, least adulterated by human habitats. The tough part of the driving was staying within the speed limit though. The roads were excellent but due to mountainous terrain it had a speed limit of 100 miles per hour. Our car would zip beyond 100 in no time and it was a constantly painful watch to check the speedometer for over speeding. We were told that the speed guns were installed at various places en route and they would easily catch anyone going beyond the limit. After sometime the driving was so boring - we were used to so much of challenges in Indian driving and here we were driving at deserted roads. All along 1200 km of driving, like a true follower of rule we never crossed the stipulated limit but were surprised to see being overtaken always, by other cars. They were surely going beyond the stipulated limit without any fear. While discussing this with our Kiwi colleagues later we learned that *"over-speeding is okay - you just have to know where the speed guns are".*

Scenic water body - New Zealand

New Zealand is one of the safest countries in the world. It has also one of the highest standards of living. It is not as multicultural - understandably because it is in the middle of nowhere geographically. For the small population it has, it offers a great peaceful lifestyle.

I recall one incident of the fire-alarms fitted in the multi-storied apartment. One of our colleagues staying there for longer time, used to cook food at home. Most of the Indians, I have found can't live away from their Indian food for long, even in a foreign country. Indian preparations with the oil do produce some smoke at times. He would have never imagined that it would trigger a fire alarm. Once the alarm was triggered the entire complex needed to be vacated without fail. The surprising part of the whole incident was the hefty fine imposed by the fire police to trigger the false alarm. After this incident he would advise everyone - *"never cookparathas in your apartment in Wellington, it will trigger afire alarm".* We were discussing later jokingly, whether a small deliberate fire would have made sense to escape the huge fine, once the alarm was triggered. Anyway the next task for my colleague was to remove the battery from the alarm switch but the fear of the alarm trigger again was too much of a risk.

Chapter 7

Asian region and city states - Emerging nations on world stage

Singapore

For anyone who visits Singapore for the first time, he or she can't remain unimpressed with this city. I have been there many times and have also stayed for a longer duration. I can surely say this country is quite unique in many ways. It is small, rather tiny island of 40X60 km (if one drives for 2 hour continuously he or she would reach the border of the country either way) but as systematic and orderly as one can imagine. The airport is one of the best airports in the world with an airline best known for its high standard of service. Singapore airlines is a dass apart when it comes to international airlines, almost better than most of the western airlines. For the city state, it is one of the most proud brand, no wonder Singapore airlines was the first airline to incorporate A380 into its fleet and first airport to fly it. The airline and the airport is a good preamble to the kind of country Singapore is.

Once into the city, the order and systematic planning is visible everywhere. This is much evolved country that way -1 have not seen so much of the town planning and dvic sense anywhere else. There are no advertisements and billboards on the roadsides and it is true for most part of the city. The reason for banning the same is, that they spoil the aesthetic sense. The houses are systematically built; to me they looked like as perfect as an architect would model it for display. It is hard to believe that it is a living city where people live with so much of systematic structures and planning. The houses were predominantly built by the Housing Development Board which is a government body. The public housing in Singapore is considered to be one of the most successful housing policies in the world. The government has created good number of multi-storied houses that are suffident for most of the population at a very affordable price. The common saying in Singapore is - irrespective of the economic status, everyone has a house, mostly built by government. So there is nothing like shantytowns or individuals building the houses to their own fancy. Almost all of them are multi-storied well planned housing complexes. This really gives a sense of order to the city unlike any other city. The public infrastructure is really commendable. The city's skyline is all full of skyscrapers. The average height of the building here is one of the maximum in the world. Living in one of these tall building may not be as comfortable though. I was living on the 32nd floor of a tall building and I can remember, how the fully packed glass building was so airtight that it was suffocating at times.

Searching house for rent was a big challenge for us. Our house broker said that most of Chinese house owners were not very keen to rent their houses to Indians. The reason, I was told about was quite weird - that Indians cook at home and they cook spicy food. The spicy food spoils the kitchen, according to the Chinese house owners. The spices from the food get stuck to the kitchen wall, they used to say. Finally we found one Indonesian who was willing to rent his house to us. After renting his house he left for Jakarta with his entire family and house goods. Later I understood that he gamed the system by availing easy house loan from government and he had stopped paying the installments. He would conveniently ask me to transfer rent electronically. After few defaults, there were police warrants against him and they would frequent our house. The police checked our papers and asked us to inform in case we got any call from the house owner. We somehow completed the lease term and changed the house. The remarkable thing about the whole incident was the extreme politeness with which the police representatives would deal with us, knowing that we were not at fault. The police person would politely explain the whole situation and ask for permission and right time to visit the house. In Singapore, I realized the police can be polite and effective at the same time unlike what we see in India. Once a friend of mine told me in Singapore - *"you don't need to be scared of police here, many times they act as good counsel"*.

Singapore is a 'fine' city, is the popular saying there. The 'fine' means 'penalty' and there are host of reasons that includes having chewing gums and feeding birds, for which fines can be levied. It is not only the formation of these rules but their strict enforcement that is the characteristic of this city. For foreigners, it is always a fear that they do not land up on the wrong side of the law. The legal system allowed for a lesser degree of punishment for the foreigners than the citizens for similar offence. Other than the usual punishments for offences, Singapore is also famous for 'caning' its offenders. What was surprising was that the caning is done mechanically, where an iron cane of certain length and weight hits at a spedfied momentum. Hence each caning is expected to cause fixed pain. This was the extreme mechanization in my view. If the offender couldn't bear all the caning at one go - he is taken to hospital for recovery and once he recovers the remaining number of caning is done. There was a notorious inddent of an American teenager who used to spray white paints on the parked vehicle in the streets. After lot of surveillance through hidden camera he was caught and awarded caning. There was lot of noise made about it in American media but Singapore, known for its law enforcement, did not deter from it.

Drug peddling is a crime punishable by death in Singapore like few other South East Asian countries. Singapore had one of highest death penalty rate in proportion to the population. The remarkable thing is their enforcement of the rule of law. Sometime back, an Australian was found guilty of peddling drugs in Singapore and was handed over death penalty. Amid multiple protest the Singapore Prime Minister remarked *"The Australian press is very colorful but the law of land should prevail"* - this he said after the offender was executed. The normal offence could be challenged in the higher court but if the defendant lost, the punishment increased further. The legal provisions were perfect living condition for the law abiding citizens. The sense of security that I had in Singapore was unparalleled. Anytime of the day or night Singapore is perfectly safe.

Even with the sense of security and safety not many would agree that Singapore encourages voices of dissent in political or social system. There has been one and only one significant political party in existence so far. In the name of democratic opposition there are typically one or two people who get elected. The people in government and police are more powerful than others. The common citizens do not have too many things to complain about, so even the monopolistic single party democracy is acceptable. During my two years stay there, I never saw a single public demonstration which we were so used to seeing in a country like India. This meant that people were either too happy or have got used to this.

I learned that in response to the criticism for not encouraging differing political view, the government started what they called 'Speaker's Corner'. It was a small identified public place where people had to first register and then speak against any government policies that they chose. The audience was not guaranteed and the entire incident might be getting monitored as well. Even the discerning views should be expressed in certain permitted ways at certain time under some vigilance and predictably the speaker's corner was a deserted place mostly. I think the people have learned to live with this and appreciate the good governance and prosperity that the government continues to deliver, more than the voices of dissent and confrontation.

As a tourist destination - Singapore is a great example in how well it has marketed itself. It is a small country and is not privileged to have great natural sight or places of historical importance. One week will be good enough to see all the prominent places there. It is one of the most tourist friendly city with good tourism infrastructure, everything is well organized and packaged well. Many of the tourist spots are artificially created. I was pleasantly surprised to experience the cold of Snow city in the sweltering climate there. Even for the places like Sentosa or Night safari - it is more of the innovative concept, packaging and marketing. Overall I always felt that the country was slightly overrated as a tourist destination.

Merlion - Sentosa Island, Singapore

For the western expatriates, this is the best country to have a first-hand experience in Asia. It has a good blend of Asian values with modern amenities and best in class infrastructure, better than many of the western cities. The safety and security conditions are far better than most of the western cities. No wonder many western expatriates choose it as a favored work location in Asia. English is well spoken and understood widely, though in slightly characteristic Singlish way. Probably Singapore could be most cosmopolitan city in Asia, but it is too good to be called a representative Asian city. It is a case of isolated excellence and most of the other cities in Asia are significantly different. Many of the public policies like housing, public transport are best implemented there.

The local underground tube system called MRT is probably the best in the world. It is well planned, regulated, maintained and covers the entire city easing much of the traffic on the roads. The government has implemented a number of measures to control the number of cars on the road. The certificate of entitlement scheme is to regulate the number of car every year on the roads. The extent to which such planning and implementation can go there is really praiseworthy. Each of the multi-storied apartment complex built by the government are allocated as per the stipulated ethic mix viz. Chinese, Malay and Indians. This is to maintain good social harmony and prevent any pockets of ethnic concentration. Some of these planning really show lot of foresight.

There is a sizable Indian population in Singapore, mostly from southern India. Most of them are early settlers and have very little commonality or do not identify much with the mainstream Indians today. To the comfort of the Indians, there was a small place called 'Little India' where many Indians could feel at home - there was no rule there, the rush and chaos symptomatic of a typical Indian city. Most of these Indians were blue collar unskilled workers who did not live in great conditions. There were incidents of some riots in this area sometime back which was unprecedented in Singapore, given its peaceful and law abiding nature. It is only off-late in last 10 years that the white collar workers of Indian origin have started frequenting Singapore.

One of my friend once said that the two fastest growing cities in India these days are Dubai and Singapore. It could be true - Singapore could be ideal choice for Indian wanting to work abroad. As an Indian, one will never feel out of place there. Unlike many cities of the west, it is closer to India (as good as living in a different city), has all the modern amenities, great infrastructure and above all an equitable and safe environment. It also has some of the problems of developed economy like high cost of living. One of my friends living there said he always preferred to get treated in India for any medical or healthcare issues. In Singapore, half of the times the doctors would not have seen the kind of diseases (on a lighter note) that Indians would have had and would be twice as costly also. No one can blame them for that, after all they don't have contaminated water and food and different varieties of mosquitoes to infect our immunity systems. Once a friend fell ill and was suspected of Malaria - he had visitors from Ministry of health who conducted an investigation after cordoning off the area. Healthcare facilities in Singapore are one of the best in Asia.

Skyline from Boat Quay - Singapore

Historically Singapore has remained a prominent port city. It was governed as a British colony and has been strategically important for the trade and military purposes. It was part of Malaysia when the British were thrown out in 1963, in line with many other disappearing colonies. Two years later Singapore separated from Malaysia as a country in its current form. The growth of Singapore since then has been hallmark of the good public polides adopted by its government. It is due to those carefully planned and implemented policies that Singapore is well integrated into the world economy and one of the most prosperous nations having high per capita income. It has adopted open market polices and registered high GDP growth year on year, thus creating a prominent financial hub in Asia. The strength and weakness of this country is its size. It is so well governed due to its small size and its independent growth and influence in the world will always be restrained due to its size.

For all its merits and advantages, Singapore to me was a beautiful box. It looked good and attractive but there was a sense of synthetic beauty in it. I am told that out of many people who grow up in the country, a significant proportion want to settle outside. It could be only natural; for all the rules and artificial surrounding, it could be limiting at times too. A cheerful and healthy life may need more natural setup, less fettered by so many rules and planning. At some point it contradicts the freedom and creativity that people are entitled to. So whether it is a good place to settle, people can have differing views; but for a short stay of work and to experience a different way of life, Singapore is surely refreshing.

One more thing that I found remarkable about Singapore, was people being so polite and respectful in general. Even during the situation of confrontation, they would be calm and talk peacefully. I recall once I was walking on the sidewalk of a busy road. Suddenly, I saw a car speeding and banging into the front car. The cars were badly damaged, luckily no one was hurt in the accident. Next moment the drivers of the two cars came out, shook hand first and greeted each other. They spoke for few minutes, shared their cards and left. There was no altercation and shouting at each other. I can't ever imagine an incident like that in India. It also denotes the faith that people have in the system rather than taking it upon themselves.

Malaysia

The tourism tagline of 'Malaysia - truly Asia' to some extent is correct. Asia is largely chaotic, economically not so well off with some pockets of excellence. Unlike Singapore, Malaysia is more close to representing complexity and disparity amongst its masses. While travelling by a bus from Singapore, if one has to make a guess which side of the boarder he is - he will always be right. The Singapore side of the boarder will be well lit, all the lights working, roads well done and roadside trees properly trimmed and maintained. The Malaysian side will be far from perfect, no way comparable to the previous ones. The same is not true if one travels by air. The Airport at Kuala Lumpur is equally good and comparable to any other airport in the world. Once into the city, it is not much different from any of the Indian cities. A typical street in Kuala Lumpur may look very similar to a place in Chennai. Due to the bigger size, most of the city is not as well planned as some pockets. Going by that logic small is more uniform and manageable. The influence of public planning greatly reduces as the size of the country increases, that can be construed as an applicable principle for most of the Asian countries including India and China.

KLCC Twin Tower - view at night

Petronas twin tower used to be the tallest structure in the world till 2004. The 88 floor structure is one of the marvelous sight of modern architecture, especially when it is lit in bright white light and adorns the skyline of Kuala Lumpur. It was constructed as a symbol of the national pride of Malaysia. It has a sky bridge connecting the twin towers, the top view from there is spectacular. The structure of KLCC is used as shopping complex for bottom few floors. These were some of the most modern shops with all high-end brands exhibited. It looked like very upscale shopping complex, one of the costliest for tourists looking for good buys. Other than the pride of having the tallest structure and getting into records, I am not sure if they are really commercially viable projects.

One of the weekends, I travelled to Genting highland, a very popular tourist destination in Malaysia. It was one of the first few theme parks setup in the beautiful hills. The place is an hour drive from KL and also accessible through cable cars. When I had first visited sometime in 2006, I had never been to such massive entertainment park. Those days the concept of theme parks in India had still not picked up. The place had large indoor and outdoor section with lot of cultural programs, all kind of rides and some water sports. It is a must visit place for holidays with friends and families. Within KL, city there are city tours that covers national mosque, palaces and museums. The tour packages are quite convenient and very well organized, sign of a country with good tourism infrastructure.

During my first visit to Malaysia in 2006, I definitely felt it was more developed than India in those days. Compared to India, the GDP per capita has been significantly higher in Malaysia, one of the richest South East Asian country. Malaysia was one of the countries that grew significantly during 80s and 90s, along with other south East Asian city states. Their currency Malaysian Ringgit has been one of stable and stronger ones. First time I saw the paper currency that was crush proof and water proof. I still remember how one of my friend crushed a currency note several time but it came back to its original shape within few seconds. Compared to the half torn dirty currency notes that we were used to seeing in India, it was a surprise for the first time.

One very interesting thing there I found was the way the local Bahasa Malaysia was written. It is the predominant language in Malaysia. Malaysia was a British colony earlier but the English language was degraded in favor of Bahasa. Some of the shops would be marked as "ais krim shop" - which actually meant "Ice Cream shop". Similarly the pharmacy shops would be marked as "farmasi". I understood it was a phonetic translation of English words in Bahasa. I am sure it would be challenging for the kids in the spell bee competitions there.

One of the noticeable things in Malaysia, were the cars on the road. While most of the car industry in different countries were dominated by Japanese, German and American cars; Malaysia had its own version called 'Proton'. Most of the cars on the roads were Proton cars. I have never seen such cars outside, so it was little surprising. I learned Proton had a long history, it was supported by the government to promote indigenous production. The foreign cars had high excise duty to make the local cars more competitive. It could be a good case study on whether the protectionist policies themselves can drive industry growth in a country. I wondered if it was something similar to the Ambassador story in India. However, Proton was quite successful and has evolved with time; it is not as disastrous as the Indian example. Malaysia is also gifted with good oil reserve. It has been a hub for electronic goods production.

Thailand

When I first visited Bangkok in 2003, it was my first visit to any South East Asian country then. I was very impressed with the infrastructure there - the swanky airport, sky train, expressways, shopping malls. Those were the days when India had probably none of these. Going through these structures, I wondered how come India missed this infrastructure revolution while even the smaller south East Asian countries did so well. These countries adopted an export oriented growth in manufacturing, attracting good foreign investment. India on the contrary was just emerging from a long era of protectionist policies that promoted license raj and import substitution. Some of these smaller countries like Thailand were more open to market economy and did much better relatively.

Bangkok was also one the best place buy *'quality fake products'*. These counterfeit products were available at select street markets and also the malls at times, at a fraction of original cost. Such markets, I knew existed in most of the countries but Bangkok I believe, was more notorious for the same. These items were also quite popular for the backpackers from west who would come on shoe string budget. Once one of my friend shared his experience of buying a Rolex watch in one of these market. He was given a rate card with the brand names. One could buy any brand with a fraction of the original brand price. The items looked so real that even the original manufacturer could not distinguish at times.

After he bought the Rolex watch for some few hundred Bhat, it went out of order when he came to Bangalore. He claimed that he went to the Rolex showroom in Bangalore and got it repaired for free, as even the licensed shop owner could not detect it was fake. It seems the fake manufacturers also successfully copy the unique identifier code that the original manufacturers use, to distinguish the original items.

The night life in Bangkok is one of the main tourist attraction. The streets are lined up by well-lit night clubs and bars in some of these areas. The place is very lively as many of these night clubs will be operational late night and carry out many performances. The place was no less remarkable than what I saw in similar area of Amsterdam. The city is pretty safe for tourists, even to roam around late night. In general the cost of living is very moderate thus making Bangkok an affordable tourist destination for Indians. Thai massage is quite popular as well and one would find numerous such massage centers that would be operational day and night. They would put up characteristic blinking tiny bulbs in front of each such massage centers.

First few days of my stay, I recall, I had some inconvenience with the local food. Though I had eaten Thai food in India before, the authentic Thai food in Thailand did not suit my palate as much. I also recall the very different aroma at the food courts. I was told that it was because of excessive sea food and the kind of oil they used to cook. I know lot of Indians relished these food but I did have difficulty in adjusting to it.

I ended up surviving on mac burgers, chocolates and other snacks. The local food is primarily rice, sea food and non-veg dishes. Amongst vegetarian item I recall tofu was quite common. It was like Indian paneer but somehow I thought it tasted quite differently.

Bangkok used to have very infamous traffic jams during peak hours. I remember long hours of waiting at times. Though the traffic is bad in almost all large cities, Bangkok situation was quite worse. Once a taxi driver told us that many of them used to keep "urination bag" in the cars as they would be stuck for hours at time. I am not sure if it was really true, or I misunderstood his narration and broken English. English was not commonly understood well so it would be difficult to communicate at times. The city had good public transport infrastructure like roads and sky trains.

China

I had a short 3 week visit to China sometime in 2010. It was to a city called Shenzhen which was dose to Hong Kong. So I took a taxi from Hong Kong Airport to Shenzhen. I crossed the border security checkpoint which was not a straightforward process and I recall several questions being asked before the immigration dearance. Shenzhen is one of the prominent financial hubs in China. It was setup as spedal economic zone by the government and the city received huge foreign direct investment. It was one of the fastest growing cities in the world in 1990s. The city very well captured the growth that China had, post opening of its economy. It captures the China model of economic growth very well. It has impressive skyline, full of tall housing and business structures. The city had one of the best infrastructures in public transport, roads etc. - surely an example of a planned city at a much large scale and symbol of Chinese development.

One can be sure that he or she has arrived in China when most of the common social media sites and search engines stop working. People in China have their own version of Facebook, Twitter, WhatsApp that are popular there. However for most of the international travelers and immigrants, I am sure this is one of the greatest inconvenience. Many of the commonly used sites start throwing error or hang up with weird messages. The internet that we take so much granted for free, is restricted there. I am not sure to what extent a country today could benefit by blocking its citizen from providing unrestricted access to internet. This kind of control also captures the approach of China in several other policies. Thanks to these government overreach on their citizens, one can start missing the basic democratic values and freedom of speech.

Those were the hyper growth years of Chinese economy when it was growing at the rate of 9-10%, the fastest in the world. It was surprising however that during my informal conversation with local colleagues, most believed that the government data were not accurate and they were inflated. It seemed most of the Chinese did not believe the public data were real, be GDP or inflation. It was all carefully engineered. Also, my previous understanding of China was that it was probably one of the least corrupt country due to strict government rules. The Chinese that I met, again believed that the government and army officials in particular did take advantage of their positions resulting into similar corruption like we have in India.

One of the most memorable experience there was the team lunch that we used to have with our colleagues. In the team of 10-12 people there were rotating roles like "CFO (chief food officer)" and "CEO (chief entertainment officer). The role of the CFO was to prearrange a different restaurant every week with the group booking for lunch. The lunch would typically be served on a large rotating round table where scores of dishes will be served one by one. It was one of the liveliest way of having the lunch together while most of the food items would be shared just like typical buffet. The role of the CEO was to pre-book an entertainment joint or some outing on the Friday afternoon.

Most of my colleagues had nice sleek mobile phones. I had the old style blackberry which looked like blunt instrument at times. I recall one of my friends commenting if what I was carrying as a phone was for personal safety (can be used as stone to hit someone in case of emergency)? The range of mobile phones available there were really surprising. Chinese mass manufacturing has created a unique place for itself in the world. Incidentally, China also has a dubious reputation of copying almost anything, mass producing at a fraction of the cost and later exporting it to the country where it originated. The difference between Chinese and Indian growth model has been predominantly that. While China's growth was fueled by mass manufacturing, India's growth post liberalization has been services led. China, of course had the massive head-start on market economy based growth and India has a lot to catch up. Most of the Chinese, I noticed would dismiss India as any significant challenge on any aspect be it economic, political or national security.

One thing that Chinese could beat Indians or may be as competitive, was when it came to long hours of work. When I travelled to western countries, I had the impression that Indians had that advantage of always willing to work extra hours (which is not necessarily healthy) thus outpacing many of their local peers. Chinese could give a tough fight to this behavior of Indians. Some of these are Asian traits I believe that even Korean and Taiwanese exhibit.

On the last day of my return from Shenzhen I recall, I left my bag inside a taxi while I was going to the office. As a daily routine, I used to hire taxi to go to the office in the morning. I had planned to leave for the airport directly from the office that evening. It was a city taxi that I had picked outside the hotel from main road. I forgot to pick my bag from the taxi once I reached the office. Later I realized that all my travel documents including passport were in the bag. I really got panicked as I had no trace of the taxi and it was not from any taxi company. I just had few hours to trace back the taxi and get my stuff back. Relating to a similar situation in India, I thought it was almost impossible to get back my bag. Luckily I discovered the small receipt that the taxi driver had given when I had paid the bill. It had a centralized number. My friend called up the number and within next two hours the bag was delivered back to me well before the travel. I was happy and relieved but wondered if in any other country I would ever have got it back so easily - definitely not India.

While discussing with some of the Chinese friend there, I understood China had a peculiar rule for the land purchase right. As per the communist government, all land belonged to state and hence collectively to the people. Individuals or companies could only purchase the right to use the land for a varying period of 20-70 years, they could not own the land. Also, such rights were give only for specified purpose and could be withdrawn if violated. I found this rule quite unique, I am sure there would be extensive legal framework to govern that. China had many unique rules including something like 'one child policy'. The rules are also very strictly implemented. I was told how once a couple applied for a permission to have their second child as their first child was 'autistic'. The permission was denied as no exceptions were encouraged. This rule is relaxed now but my sense was that most of the Chinese were not happy about the restrictions in different spheres of their personal and social lives.

Hong Kong

I used to travel to Hong Kong on a frequent basis for a year or so. All these were short business trips. Hong Kong used to provide (now they have withdrawn I understand) a 15 day stay visa on arrival to Indians. This was also the reason possibly that I would often see many of Indian families going there for holidays. Some of them would be quite boisterous while travelling in the group. They would have fun in their way at times causing inconvenience to other passengers.

One of the biggest disappointments in Hong Kong used to be the hotel rooms for the sheer small size and compactness. Land is very short in availability there, so they have very innovative ways to create smaller rooms, more so the bathrooms. Many of these hotel rooms would not have windows and may appear claustrophobic. The general housing is also similar, it is highly improbable to spot an apartment that does not have at least more than 20 floors. Hong Kong can only grow vertically. The average height of building would be probably be one of the highest in in the world.

Hcmg Kong Skyline from hill tram on way to Victoria Peak

Hong Kong is part of China now - a special administrative zone. It was the last remnant of British Empire till 1997. The peaceful handover of the region to China is case study on how China leveraged its influence to virtually push the British in a corner for control of this colonial region. As a diminishing world power Britain could hardly maneuver anything but complete transfer of power to China. This history explains how Hong Kong evolved as one of the most dynamic trading and electronics manufacturing hub at par with the most developed cities in the world. It had all the advantages of a sustained high economic growth along with freedom and liberty which was restricted in China.

Hong Kong has its own currency and its own set of laws different from China under what they called "one country - two systems". The paranoia of the Chinese handover was so much, that when the iconic 47 storied HSBC building was built in 1970s, it consisted of moveable parts that were assembled there. Apparently the reason was - should the need arise, the entire building could be dismantled and shifted to Britain. It is one of the masterpiece in the new age architecture. It is lit beautifully in orange and white light at night.

A very characteristic thing about Hong Kong is the way it is lit-up every night. Almost all of its tall sky scrapers would display beautiful colors, sometimes advertisements as well. It is also called world's most light polluted city with number of LED lights and billboards. There have been campaigns to reduce the level of night lighting in Hong Kong but for tourists it is a great sight while travelling in the taxi along the long coastlines. Unlike China, Hong Kong has a large English speaking population, so it is quite convenient for the tourists. It is also one of the safest cities in the world with a high standard of living.

Indonesia

One of the most remarkable things about Jakarta I remember, was their airport which looked so different but very classy. It looked like a holiday resort with multiples cottages interconnected. It was sometime during 2005-6 that I travelled there. It did not look like an airport when compared to other international airports. They had lot of small domestic airlines. Indonesian airlines were notorious for poor safety standards and increasing accidents. The situation turned so bad that at some point EU banned all of the Indonesian airlines. The things have definitely improved after that. They have got a new airport with state of the art facilities and better safety standards for their airlines. For Indians, it was visa on arrival with some brief formalities.

I recall my travel from airport to the hotel. The roads were excellent. The skyline was filled up with lot of half made structures. It looked as if the work on those structures had stopped for many years. Many of them were really big skyscrapers but in dilapidated condition. That was the decade after the Asian currency crisis of 1997 and the impact was visible all throughout the city. The decade before the crisis, the "miracle economies of Asia" also called Asian Tigers, saw huge foreign investments. It was the period marked by a boom in all economic activities. The crisis started with the currency devaluation in Thailand but Indonesia was the hardest hit due to political and social instability. The crisis led to the abrupt exit of foreign investment leading to free fall of currency. I had read about the currency crisis during our management studies but seeing the physical impact of half constructed building, I could well imagine the impact was very deep and damaging.

The hotel was fitted with multiple security barricades. This was when and terrorist attacks were less frequent in the other parts of the world. However, Indonesia had many of these attacks led by separatists and local militia. Some of these attacks were targeted at western tourists at the hotels and night clubs. This affected the safety perception of Indonesia as tourist destination and the police took extra precaution of putting multiple security barricades on most of the important buildings. Things have greatly improved subsequently.

Indonesia is a unique country, has thousands of islands. The count of these islands varies based on the counting methodologies. Most of the islands are not inhabited. Some of them appear only during the tidal period or when the waves recede. The unique geography and a rich historical background makes Indonesia a good tourist destination in Asia.

Indonesia has strong historical linkages with India. Even in the ancient Indian scriptures, Java (Yawadwipa) is mentioned. The Indian epic of Ramayana and

Mahabharata are still common in some parts. Though the country is majority Muslim today, it had clear historical linkage with Hinduism. Some of its area like Bali have strong Indian footprint e.g. Hindu temples. I read about Bali Yatra, one of the most popular festivals in Odisha that is commemorated as a ritual every year as a mark of respect for the sailors who would go to Bali on long voyage centuries ago. It depicted the strong trading and entrepreneurial focus in ancient India and connect they had with Indonesia.

The street scene is no different from a typical street in Delhi. I saw monkeys on the road, usual heavy traffic and busy streets, very symptomatic of the chaos of a rapidly growing economy. In restaurants there was restriction on the use of alcohol, I am not sure if it was banned. Indonesia had been resisting internal pressure to ban the production, distribution or consumption of alcohol. It also had a severe drug consumption problem. It starts with the grave warning in flight announcement for anyone entering Indonesia. In spite of severe punishments if caught, drug trafficking continues to be a big problem for the law enforcement there.

Sri Lanka

During my first visit to Sri Lanka, I was supposed to travel to Colombo in the week just after the Tsunami of 2004. It was a massive catastrophe that killed more than 30,000 people in Sri Lanka and several other thousands in many countries including India. It was characterized as the deadliest tsunami of the world. The images of sea shores and houses getting washed over, were playing out on TV everywhere. The hotel "Taj Samudra" that I had booked for staying, was near the sea shore (as the name signified). Fortunately that area was not affected at all. After detailed evaluation of the threat situation, I continued with my travel plan.

The hotel was right next to sea but water had receded, anyway this area was not affected. One of the advantages of travelling to south Asian countries are that one can expect very good hotels with spacious rooms at a very affordable price. My hotel experience in western countries has been quite the opposite. Most of the times it would be a small room, sometimes with no windows but exorbitantly costly. Colombo being a tourist destination looked very warm and hospitable to its guests.

My first impression of Colombo was that it was quite similar to a city like Chennai in India. The streets, shops even the restaurants looked very familiar. The familiar sights on the road, were the Indian autos look alike. Even food-wise it had lot of similarity with Indian cuisines. One can easily get a *masala dosa* in the local restaurants. The local Sinhalese population has a long history and rich culture of their own. During my conversation I recall they said lot of Indians were in business and they were regarded very well. The city looked quite structured and deaner. Colombo is one of the popular tourist destination in South Asia, it has good tourism infrastructure. The city was, by and large safe with good law and order. The exception those days were some area where the separatist movement was on the peak with violent incidents. With the end of those movements now, I am sure Sri Lanka would be one of the peaceful countries in South Asia.

A Buddhist Temple in Colombo

I went to visit one of the famous Buddhist temple called Gangaramya Temple. The architecture of the temple looked like a mix of Chinese, Indian and Thai temples. It had large number of Buddha's statues, the main one being a beautiful yellow color statue inside the temple. The temple was very close to a big lake thus adding to the serenity and calmness of the surrounding. Though Buddhism originated in India, it spread in other Asian countries more significantly. Buddhism is the religion of majority of Sri Lankans having large number of monasteries. As per historical records, Buddhism was introduced to Sri Lanka by son of King Asoka way back in third century BC. The subsequent kings supported this further and adopted as a way of life. It is a subject matter of deeper research why Buddhism which originated in India and was adopted as main religion in many of the Asian nations, did not flourish as much in India.

Sri Lanka is gifted with beautiful flora and fauna. Along with long coastline it has beautiful mountains and hills that are good trekking area for nature lovers. Kandy hills were one of the most popular centers of attraction. It was an old hill city with lot of historical structure. It has a temple which is believed to house the tooth relic of Buddha.

Sri Lanka is also famous for good textiles at affordable prices. When I went there earlier in 2005, it had a small airport as bad as one of the Indian cities. There were hardly any shopping space at the airport. On subsequent visits recently, I found their new terminals expansive and world dass with lot of shopping area, something very important for Colombo for their tourists. Indians had visa on arrival, one of the very few countries to offer this privilege to Indians. It can be an excellent destination for family holidays for Indians - affordable and great value for money.

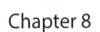

Chapter 8

Latin America - Yet to be discovered by Indians

Argentina

Latin America has been an exotic location for me - it is such a large continent with many countries and large population, but little is talked about it. In proportion, even Africa gets far more coverage in the international media and discussions. It is a lesser known continent, in our part of the world. They are not known for wealth, not known for poverty either, and politically they are not so interconnected with the world too. They have fewer incidents making news headlines worldwide - I presume they were somewhat a different world of their own.

So, my first visit to Buenos Aires was something that I was quite looking forward to, a different an interesting part of the world. By then, the most I had heard about Argentina was with respect to the football world cup and from a movie "Evita", particularly the song *"Don't cry for me Argentina"*. The air journey was one of longest from India and with a 14 hour transit in Milan; it could be one of the most inconvenient route to reach. The flight from Milan to Buenos Aires was another 14 hours, one of longest end to end journey time for me. The connectivity also showed that very few people from India travel to that part of the world.

An art shop in Buenos Aires

I had read about the night life in Buenos Aires as being one of the liveliest and it turned out to be true. If one did not carry the watch one would never know whether it was late evening or early morning. Once, we saw one lady walking with her kids with school bags on; when we looked at the watch, it was 3 am in the morning. We kept wondering if people had the sense of timing there, especially on weekends. Many parts of the city turned into a partying hub during weekends and we were told that the weekend promptly started on Thursday evening for the majority. For the next three days in the week it was only partying. If one had to pick up the most conspicuous things in their social life, partying would be one of them. During one of the discussion I learned that people were so obsessed with partying that they would put on thick curtain on the windows to avoid seeing the sunlight and continue their night binge in the pubs. It was one of the few countries where I saw women would mostly outnumber the men in those pubs. We met an Indian who was living in Argentina for a long time. His view was - unlike India you could go and talk to any of those girls, offer them drink and have discussions. To prove that point in the pub he said - he would go and talk to some of the ladies there without any hesitation. He went and accosted some of them asking *"do you speak English"*. Many of them just responded saying "no" in sign or in words. He kept trying though, finally he got one response with a smile *"I speak English but don't want to speak now"*. My friend still took it as corroboration of his statement. People are quite approachable in general but one must know Spanish for that because English was hardly a common language there.

Buenos Aires looked a fairly structured and well-developed city. The infrastructure was good, they had wide roads. It had an underground rail system which looked a bit dated but efficient. The economy had been quite unstable though. During one of the conversations a local friend explained about the plight of Argentinian economy - *"when god created Argentina, He gave all the riches, wealth, fertile land, minerals, long coastline every thing. Along with all this the God created Argentinians who would self-destruct themselves every few years"*.

There is a famous quote by a Nobel laureate - *"there are four kind of countries in the world: developing countries, developed countries, Argentina and Japan"*. By this he probably meant that due to weird policies and abrupt changes, Argentina had brought crisis to itself after every patch of good growth. It was one of the top ten rich country in the world not long ago. The great depression of 1998-2002 was something that people still talked about with painful memories. My friend explained the impact on job, social lives etc. when the economy shrank by more than a quarter. It was one of biggest social crisis for them.

One of the common remembrance of a typical marketplace or square in Buenos Aires I have, is of tango dance. These were the street performances. A small troupe of performers will pair up in couple and perform mesmerizingly to an audience. It would be a young man and woman but kids also joined at times. It would be synched up well with the music played on a local instrument. They would ask for money at the end of the show like typical street performers.

Walking through the public park could well be an unusual sight at times. From the outset, Argentina looked far less conservative than many other countries that I have visited. Women were equally visible in most public places and there was general sense of good law and order. It had large number of gay and lesbians bars, perhaps one of the most progressive cities in that sense. Same sex marriage is legalized there now.

First discussion in the office was always about the football match of the previous night. In case one missed it, well no one misses it seems. The Argentines follow their football team very earnestly, much more passionately and universally than the Indians who follow their cricket team. It is not surprising that world over most people would co-relate Argentina with football. They have also produced some of the legendry players in football.

I don't think there were any significant number of Indian immigrants unlike many other countries. Their knowledge about India and its culture was also limited. I remember during one of the conversation I was asked *"I hear there are cows commonly found on the Indian roads - don't you have farms?"* I responded - *"other than cows we also have dogs and monkeys as often found on the roads and other public areas"*. Due to the long distance and language problems, Argentina is still one of the most unexplored country by Indians. The city was popular with Europeans for holidays and vacations.

Venezuela

When I landed at Caracas Airport, I recall how difficult it was for me to even step outside and find a taxi. I had been to Spanish speaking countries earlier and I always had the confidence that I can manage little bit. But Caracas was entirely different, I could not even explain a word. We waited for our Spanish speaking colleague to arrive who was expected by another flight few hours later. We realized that had he not come as scheduled, we would have been in a difficult situation and stuck at the airport itself. All during our stay in Caracas, I never stepped out unless I was with someone who knew Spanish. I was also told it was not very safe for foreigners if they did not know the local language. I can well imagine why there were so few Indians there. Other than the country being so far off, the language problem would scare the immigrant Indians who even tried to venture.

Venezuela is famous for the Miss Worlds, as we mostly know. When I was speaking to some of the folks there in informal discussion, they told that this obsession for beauty contests had gone to clinical level in many cases. There were girls who would prepare for these events from a very early age; they would be very particular for their food and many cases would suffer from anorexia. It was a social problem there. Many of them would not marry or marry very late as it would affect their chances at beauty contest otherwise. It was almost looking like a professional hazard. It was a surprise to me that even an innocuous thing like a beauty contest can create social issues if obsessive. It is due to these problems that some countries ban the extra thin models.

When I was walking through one of the local park, I saw a huge protest by people. I was told that it was a march for the support of then president Hugo Chavez. The supporters and protesters clashed very often and it was a quite common it seemed. Many times, these demonstrations would turn violent and it was advisable to stay away from such protests. Though the president had been in power for a long time, he had a strong opposition from people. The general law and order condition was not very good. Internationally, Venezuela has been more secluded with little integration with the rest of the world, thanks to its strong leaning towards the communist ideologies.

Hill top view in Caracas

Venezuela is one of the largest oil producers and exporters in the world. However the wealth, that is obvious in the Middle East oil producing country, is conspicuously absent in Caracas. I understand the government policies have been blamed for the ongoing economic malaise in Venezuela. It is said to be a failed experiment in socialism. The ultra-nationalistic governments have been blamed for discouraging market investments. They nationalized many of their oil companies. Nearly half of the country's GDP came from oil (which consisted nearly 100% export). With the oil prices coming down last few years the country is in serious economic trouble. Just last year they had shortage of basic amenities like milk, toilet papers etc. that forced thousands of people to cross border to Colombia to buy necessities. As per recent reports, the food items had been rationed and electricity had been cut. I saw large number of shantytowns in and around Caracas. They had small houses called Barrio that were infamous for lack of basic amenities like electricity, water or sanitation.

I remember going to Avila Mountain via cable cars. It presents a nice view of the city. The unique thing about the hill was, it separated the city from sea. It presents a nice natural view - one side was vast Caribbean Sea while the other side the expanse of the city area. This I understood was one of most popular place. The city was not easy to go around for foreigners, especially with not good enough Spanish knowledge. The security conditions also were not very conducive.

Summary: My learnings from the travels

I learned about India more by travelling abroad

It looks counterintuitive, but in reality I learned more about India while travelling abroad. Sometimes it would be trivial facts that I would be asked about while talking to local folks, like number of languages and religion India had, population and geographies of various cities etc. As I would enquire about the city population, culture, most famous things there etc. in a new city, I was asked similar questions about the country and city I came from. I realized I knew very little about my own country. So every time I discussed about a particular country, it also enriched my knowledge and appredation of the country we live in. Some basic things like scores of living languages in India is so inconceivable in many countries. In many countries people could not believe that diversity. The fact that we had so many religious beliefs was also a unique discovery though it comes very naturally to Indians. A city like Delhi was bigger than most of the European countries in population. I realized India was really diverse, noisy, big but largely peaceful and harmonious.

Some of the old Indian history has links with foreign countries. There was a time when India was one of the richest country, it was invaded and colonized. The wealth of some of these loots and war trophies could be found in museums abroad. This also raises interest in learning about our own history. One such moment was seeing 'Kohinoor' diamond in Tower of London. It has a fascinating history of its own that tells story about India's glorious past as well as subsequent decline during colonization. Even in countries like Turkey, Iran and many European countries, many Indian artifacts were preserved. India had more than 20% of the world GDP at some time, they had flourishing trade across the world. Even Buddhism that widely spread in many countries had its origin in India. Traces and links of Indian civilization can be found in many countries abroad and that can be a credible basis to study India.

What we learn from media is not always the true picture

We learn about other cultures mostly through the electronic media, be it newspapers, TV or internet. I think the media does not have an equitable representation from all cultures, countries and ways of living. Some countries dominate the world discourse through media prowess. The point of views are not always real and correct. For example I had a terrible view of Tehran before I visited them, met many people. They were one of the nicest and most warm people. They seemed to have fond connection with India and its culture. Similarly, most of the African and Latin American nations don't get reported at all.

The media that we are exposed to covers a very narrow point of view of select nations like US, UK, China, Russia etc. Most of these views do have political overtones, so the picture is also distorted when the news are reported. Hence it was always refreshing to see that there are many other interesting countries that otherwise we don't hear about. The experiential truth in most cases I have found, were different from the perception that I had about people and the place.

India was really transitioning faster than many other countries

From my first international trip in year 2000 to now, if one country has changed the most, it is India. Whether it is seen through the improved airports, new airlines or the fruits of liberal economy showing its signs - I could see the perceptible change from my first travel to now. When I travelled during earlier days, I was almost sure that India could never have an airport like Singapore or a highway in Bangkok or metro train in China. In a very short period, some of these infrastructures in India have changed and actually become world class. I, in no way conclude that all our infrastructure problems have been solved, but we have travelled considerable distance.

Another noticeable thing was the way Indians brought in foreign items earlier through customs. Due to the protectionist and import substitution policies, Indian products in 80s and 90s were one of the worst qualities from international standards. Import duties were very high on foreign brands. So it was not unusual for people to buy electronic items abroad before coming back to India. For every visit, I would get a request to buy some camera, phones or even laptops. The custom officials were the real fear at exit points. The NRI visit to their Indian relatives were the most sought after events. This has changed completely. Now I don't see people arguing with the custom authorities for buying a camera abroad. We get everything in India at the same quality if not superior. The quality of life has definitely improved in last 15 years. The consumers also have become more aware and demand quality products everywhere.

The Indian immigrants always had the umbilical cord intact

Whenever I met Indian immigrants in foreign countries, almost certainly I found them warm and easy to connect with. While we are so divided in India, when we go abroad and settle, there are very common threads to connect; be it cricket, Bollywood, food, life in India or the culture. This I found even in some countries like Mauritius where the folks migrated many generations ago. Though they have adopted the local culture excelled in business, sometimes even taken citizensh but once we scratch the surface they are still all Indi at their core. There is something about Indian Origin I am told never goes away. This is not the same case many other nationalities where people assimilate and are able to ward off their instinct to often with their country of origin. Indians have been in that way.

This provides a golden opportunity for Indi with its rich diaspora and create a mutua experience. Many of the Indian immigrants le years ago for greener pastures or to es poverty in India during 60s and 70s, have done well for themselves. Indians abroad have been highly successful in business and entrepreneurship. Many of them are still Indians at heart and well-wishers of this country. I had great experience meeting them even in some remote countries like Argentina. I think the Indian government can really do more to build bridges with this diaspora who have a psychological stake in the development of India. With India getting more prominence in the world affairs, these immigrants also feel a sense of pride while relating to it.

Basic core values in all the countries were more or less similar

When we discussed during informal sessions we realized people in general are more alike than different in different countries. Most of the people were hospitable, warm and friendly. Sometimes we were invited in their social functions and I realized that many things were quite common. The spirit of living together was stronger. Sometimes we tend to get biased by the picture presented by media but the first-hand experience had een really good. For example, I always found people in frica lot more courteous, humble and friendly contrary the perception created by what we read or hear about.

sure travelling gives a fresh perspective and kind periential learning which is not possible otherwise, the age old saying goes "Travelling makes a man t".